Avro V[

The Early Years, 1947–64

DAVID W FILDES

HISTORIC MILITARY AIRCRAFT SERIES, VOLUME 7

Front cover image: Dramatic picture of the first prototype Avro Vulcan taken in September 1953.

Back cover image: Atmospheric picture of a No 617 Squadron Vulcan with Blue Steel missile pictured at Woodford.

Title page image: Pictured is the first prototype, VX770, taken on 22 April 1955.

Contents page image: Delta wing shown at its best advantage on the first prototype Vulcan, taken in September 1953.

David W Fildes joined Hawker Siddley Aviation in 1972 after working in the advertising industry. He joined the Publicity Department at Chadderton and later moved to Woodford. This is where he found an association with the XM603 Club, and later formed the Avro Hertiage Centre, with the help of Dr Peter Summerfield and Harry Holmes. It is now known as the Avro Heritage Museum, based at Woodford, and is home to XM603, shown here in the background.

Dedication

I would like to dedicate this book to the retired members of the XM603 Club, who had worked on the Avro Vulcan XM603 at Woodford since 1985. In 2007, the club members were stood down when their numbers started to deplete, and others became too old to support the aircraft. Their legacy still continues today in the Avro Heritage Museum at Woodford, where XM603 can be seen.

I would also like to recognise the contributions made by the workforce at both Chadderton and Woodford and their dedication in producing one of the world's most iconic aircraft. Finally, to the RAF personnel who looked after the Vulcan, along with the pilots and crews who flew the mighty Vulcan.

Acknowledgements

My thanks go to my friend and colleague Harry Holmes, for his support and encouragement over the years, and to Tony Blackman, Reg Boor, Ian Lowe, and Ken Newby, who gave some invaluable advice. I would also like to thank J F Henderson for his line drawings of the Vulcan B.Mk1 and B.Mk2, Harry Nelson for the foreword, and, lastly, the Avro Heritage Museum at Woodford.

Published by Key Books
An imprint of Key Publishing Ltd
PO Box 100
Stamford
Lincs PE19 1XQ

www.keypublishing.com

The right of David W Fildes to be identified as the author of this book has been asserted in accordance with the Copyright, Designs and Patents Act 1988 Sections 77 and 78.

Typeset by SJmagic DESIGN SERVICES, India.

Contents

Hephaestus, the god of fire – especially the blacksmith's fire – was the patron of all craftsmen, principally those working with metals. He was worshiped predominantly in Athens, but also in other manufacturing centres. He was also the god of volcanoes. Later, the fire within them would represent the smith's furnace.

The Romans took Hephaestus as one of their own gods, attaching the myth and cult of their god of fire, and called him Vulcan (Volcanus).

Foreword

I am greatly honoured by having been asked to write this foreword for David Fildes' excellent examination of 'the Vulcan Years'.

My friendship with David started about the time I was reintroduced, for the third time, to the Vulcan. This occurred very soon after my arrival at Avro in early 1982. But I am getting ahead of myself.

Way before then, as a young air cadet serving with No 234 Durham City Squadron, I attended a summer camp at RAF Scampton, where we cadets were tasked with cleaning the underbelly of a huge white painted bomber. At first sight the Vulcan was awe inspiring, as any Roman God of Fire should be. I never lost that emotion, even as I later flew it operationally as a Captain on 101 Sqn from RAF Waddington, and later as an instructor at RAF Scampton. I well recall my first take-off at the Operation Conversion Unit (OCU): the noise, the acceleration, and the sheer feeling of power was amazing.

Our squadron job was to be so good that we would never be employed for real. For sure, some of us would have got through to our targets, had we ever been used in anger, but such a result would have been a global failure on a catastrophic scale. We were there to deter, and only history will judge how successful we (the crews and the aircraft) were.

Some years later, I finally arrived at Woodford in January 1982 and within a short period of time the Vulcan and I were to meet again. The occasion, of course, was the Falklands War.

I stood at a window of flight operations one Friday, with my good friend, Al McDicken — also an ex-pilot; he flew the last Vulcan to fly, XH558, on its first flight after being retired by the Royal Air Force, so that it could return to display flying for the public before being retired and put on static display. We were surprised by the arrival of a Vulcan that, unknown to us at that time, was about to be converted to an air-to-air tanker. With our backgrounds, it was inevitable that we would soon be involved. Al carried out a lot of the weapons release clearance work, while I was focused on the production delivery side.

One flight I remember very well occurred on 1 July 1982. This involved flying with Martin Withers, who had just returned from Ascension Island, for a home break after his epic bombing raid on the Falklands. Martin's job was to clear me to do in-flight refuelling. This was something I had never done with the Vulcan, as 101 Sqn was all about very low-level operations. My job was to then clear the aircraft handling at weights that it had never been flown at before. We achieved both objectives and then delivered the aircraft back to RAF Waddington all in the same flight.

The facts speak for themselves. A bomber designed for high altitude operations became a strike bomber operating at ultra-low level, and was later morphed again into a tanker. The fact that it was effective in all these roles speaks volumes for the initial concept and design team, and it should be remembered that all the original work was carried out using slide rulers. This book leads us nicely through the history leading up to the operational aircraft that I knew. It also provides an insight to the thinking and the careful 'balance' and trade-offs in engineering that were necessary to succeed in all its roles. It was a great aircraft to fly as a pilot and I consider it a privilege to have had my hands on it, in three capacities: Squadron Pilot, Instructor and, finally, as an Avro Test Pilot.

Harry Nelson, Test Pilot

Dawn of the Nuclear Age

The capabilities of nuclear fission had become widely known by early 1939, notably through the work of Otto Hahn and Lise Meitner. It was recognized that nuclear weapons could potentially be built, as explained in a letter to President F D Roosevelt sent by Albert Einstein on 2 August 1939, shown below. This led to the United States' Manhattan Project in 1942 and to the building of the world's first atomic weapon.

Sir:

Some recent work by E. Fermi and L. Szilard, which has been communicated to me in manuscript, leads me to expect that the element uranium may be turned into a new and important source of energy in the immediate future. Certain aspects of the situation which has arisen seem to call for watchfulness and, if necessary, quick action on the part of the administration. I believe therefore that it is my duty to bring to your attention the following facts and recommendations.

In the course of the last four months it has been probable — through the work of Joliot in France as well as Fermi and Szilard in America — that it may become possible to set up a nuclear chain reaction in a large mass of uranium, by which vast amounts of power and large quantities of new radium-like elements would be generated. Now it appears almost certain that this could be achieved in the immediate future.

This new phenomenon would also lead to the construction of bombs, and it is conceivable — though much less certain — those extremely powerful bombs of a new type may thus be constructed. A single bomb of this type carried by boat and exploded in a port, might very well destroy this whole port together with some of the surrounding territory. However, such bombs might very well prove to be too heavy for transportation by air.

The United States has only very poor ores of uranium in moderate quantities. There is some in Canada and the former Czechoslovakia, while the most important source of uranium is Belgian Congo.

In view of this situation, you may think it desirable to have some permanent contact maintained between the administration and the group of physicists working on chain reactions in America. One possible way of achieving this might be for you to entrust with this task a person who has your confidence and who could perhaps serve in an unofficial capacity. His task might comprise the following.

a) to speed up the experimental work, which is at present being carried on within the limits of the budgets of University laboratories, by providing funds, if such funds be required, through his contacts with private persons who are willing to make contributions for this cause, and perhaps also by obtaining the co-operation of industrial laboratories which have the necessary equipment,

I understand that Germany has actually stopped the sale of uranium from the Czechoslovakian mines which she has taken over. That she should have taken such early action might perhaps be understood on the ground that the son of the German Under-Secretary of State, Von Weizsacker, is attached to the Kaiser-Wilhelm-Institute in Berlin where some of the American work on uranium is now being repeated,

Yours very truly.
(Albert Einstein)

The British Atom Bomb

The British Government had been aware of the properties of a 'super-bomb', as outlined in Otto Frisch and Rudolf Peierls' 1941 memorandum on the effects of a uranium super bomb. Interestingly, as both were Germans, they were officially classified as 'enemy aliens'. In fact, the 1941 MAUD report, which outlined the possibility of creating a nuclear weapon, was largely based on this memorandum and influenced both American and British thinking on the production of a nuclear bomb. During World War Two, British research into a nuclear weapon was highly classified and was given the code name 'Tube Alloys'.

When work had started on the atom bomb in 1942, considerable assistance was given by the British government and physicists. The first plutonium bomb was first tested under the code name 'Trinity' on 16 July 1945, in the desert of New Mexico. It was scheduled to be dropped on Germany and specific targets had been selected, but, with the ending of the war in Europe, it was politically deemed that the war with Japan should come to an early closure. Thus, America became the first country to use such a device in anger, on 6 August 1945, when they dropped a uranium-based weapon on the Japanese city of Hiroshima.

The British venture into building an atomic weapon was for national security and political purposes. A report was prepared by William Penny in October 1946 on the validity of a nuclear weapon; as a result, the Labour Prime Minister, Clement Attlee, and a select group of cabinet ministers decided to proceed with the project on 8 January 1947 and gave it the name 'High Explosive Research'. In the meantime, the Soviet Union became the second nation to successfully test a nuclear device in August 1949.

The first test of the United Kingdom's nuclear weapon was under the code name 'Operation Hurricane' and was detonated on one of the Montebello Islands, Western Australia, on 3 October 1952. This led to the UK's first deployed nuclear weapon, the Blue Danube, in November 1953. Blue Danube started to be replaced in 1958. In the meantime, the Vulcan also used the Yellow Sun and, later, the safer Yellow Sun Mk2. The American Mk5 bomb was also made available under the project E programme. Later, the Red Beard nuclear weapon using the Red Snow physics package became operational in 1961. Blue Danube was retired in 1962.

A V Roe & Co Ltd

The Avro Company was formed in 1908, when Alliott Verdon Roe built his first biplane and, later, the more famous Triplane; he formed the company A V Roe & Co, based at Brownsfield Mill, in Manchester, along with his brother Humphrey. It was registered on New Year's Day 1910 as an aeroplane manufacturer and became a full limited company on 11 January 1913.

The company was to become popularly known as AVRO, and in World War One it produced the Type 504, which was to become the first Avro aircraft to be used on a bombing raid, when three specially converted aircraft famously attacked the Zeppelin sheds at Friedrichshafen on 21 November 1914. Large orders were received for the 504 and this meant finding new premises. These were based at Clifton Street, Manchester, and a site acquired from the nearby engineering firm Mather and Platt Limited. Later, a design and experimental department was also established at Hamble, Southampton.

Avro also had a facility at Alexandra Park aerodrome in Manchester, which was closed to air traffic on 24 August 1924. This led to the company moving to New Hall Farm at Woodford, Cheshire. This meant dismantling one of the hangars at Alexandra Park for relocation to Woodford. These premises were further expanded in the 1930s, and, in 1939, a new assembly facility and runway were built owing to a government aircraft expansion programme.

Chadderton was headquarters for Avro, and where Roy Chadwick and the Initial Project Group were based.

New premises at Newton Heath were to remain the head office for more than 20 years, before a government aircraft expansion programme developed in the late 1930s and the company was charged with setting up a new factory at Chadderton, east Manchester. Chadderton was to become the headquarters and manufacturing factory during World War Two and was the heart of Avro's wartime work, producing the world-famous Avro Lancaster bomber.

Avro also operated a large underground factory at Yeadon, Yorkshire, and for several years, the company's experimental flight was based at Ringway Airport, Manchester.

As the Avro Lancaster came into service, a service repair depot was established at Bracebridge Heath, Lincoln. The repair organisation expanded rapidly and Langar, Nottinghamshire, was opened in 1942 to cope with the rebuilding and assembly of damaged aircraft.

In 1954, a new Weapons Division was formed and based at Woodford, responsible for the design and development of a stand-off bomb, which was to be carried by the Vulcan bomber. The Weapons Division rate of expansion was considerable. During 1956, a new weapons branch was set up at Salisbury, South Australia, and technicians from Woodford were transferred to Salisbury. Later acquisitions included a design group at Harrow, and a research and development group at Chertsey, Surrey.

End of an Era

In August 1920, Crossley Motors bought a 68.5 per cent share in Avro, and, in 1928, Crossley Motors sold A V Roe & Co Ltd to Armstrong Siddeley Holdings Ltd; this led to Alliott Verdon Roe resigning from Avro and founding the Saunders-Roe Company. In 1935, Avro became a subsidiary of Hawker Siddeley Group, who, in 1963, dropped the name Avro when it became part of the Hawker Siddeley Aviation (HSA) group of companies.

As a government initiative to amalgamate and rationalise Britain's foremost aviation companies during 1977, the British Aircraft Corporation (BAC), HSA and Scottish Aviation became part of the newly formed nationalised British Aerospace. By 1999, British Aerospace PLC purchased Marconi Electronic Systems (MES), which was part of the GEC group of companies to form BAE Systems. In 2011, with the cancellation of the Nimrod MRA4 maritime patrol and attack aircraft contract, BAE Systems decided to close the Woodford and Chadderton sites. Woodford became part of a housing development and Chadderton was sold for industrial units.

Chadderton and Woodford Facilities

Above: Chadderton factory and Avro headquarters pictured in June 1958. The power station supplied heat and electricity to the factory.

Left: Woodford flight sheds.

Below: Woodford new assembly pictured in 1945; note the camouflaged factory.

1947

The origins of the Avro Type 698 can be traced back to German aerodynamicist Dr Alexandra Lippisch, who made contributions to an understanding of Delta and flying wings before and during World War Two, and to a small team of young talented engineers, who were working in the Project Office at the Chadderton factory of A V Roe & Co Ltd, which was then part of the Hawker Siddeley Group.

The Avro Project Office was headed by Chief Project Engineer Robert (Bob) N Lindley, who reported to Roy Chadwick; recently promoted to the new position of Technical Director, Roy Chadwick had joined Avro in 1911, and was responsible for some of Avro's most famous aircraft designs, which included the Lancaster bomber. Stuart Davies had taken over as Chief Designer, and would later take a larger part in the design of the Vulcan when Roy Chadwick was tragically killed on 23 August 1947, whilst taking off on a test flight from Avro's Woodford Aerodrome in the Avro Tudor 2 (G-AGSU) prototype airliner. A former Director at the Royal Aircraft Establishment (RAE), William S Farren (later Sir), joined the Avro Company as Technical Director, replacing Roy Chadwick, which gave the government added confidence in the Type 698 project.

Initial Projects Team

In 1944, Avro's General Manager, Sir Roy Dobson, who joined Avro in August 1914 with Roy Chadwick, put Stuart Davies in charge of a Special Projects Group to look at new aircraft designs for the future of the company. Davies employed Jim Floyd as Chief Project Engineer and a youthful apprentice, Bob Lindley.

In 1945, Avro had taken over the Victory Aircraft facilities at Malton Ontario, Canada, and a new company was set up known as Avro Canada. In 1946, Stuart Davies asked Jim Floyd to join the new company to work on a new jetliner; this led to Lindley being promoted to Chief Project Engineer. Lindley left Avro in 1949 to join Canadair and then went to work for Avro Canada, where he joined his colleague, Jim Floyd. Lindley had a reputation for solving engineering problems and went on to be Chief Engineer on another Delta project, the Avro Arrow. After cancellation of the Avro Arrow, he then went to the space industry in the US and later joined NASA on the Shuttle programme, becoming Director of Engineering and Operations for manned space flight.

Roy Chadwick (left) and Roy Dobson discuss the merits of the Avro York transport aircraft, a derivative of the Avro Lancaster design.

Above left: **Roy Chadwick in the drawing office at Chadderton, pictured with Chief Draughtsman Jimmy Turner (centre) and a young draughtsman, Geoff Taylor (left).**

Above right: **Chief Designer Stuart D Davies pictured here in his office at Chadderton. Due to his Cockney background, Stuart was known as 'Cock' Davies.**

Bob Lindley Recollections

The Operational Requirement for the aircraft was put to the company in December 1946, together with an invitation to tender with the closing date being February 1947, which was amended to a later date. The Project Office received their copy in January 1947, but before they were able to get very far, the great fuel shortage hit the plant and it was subsequently closed down. Bob Lindley, Head of Special Projects, and Donald Wood, Aerodynamicist, were able to get hold of an office, which had belonged to the Resident Technical Officer (RTO), to carry on their study. Another upheaval taking place at that time was that Roy Chadwick was at home suffering from shingles.

The performance requirements of the Operational Requirement were rather startling to people nurtured

Mr William S Farren (later Sir) joined Avro as Technical Director, replacing Roy Chadwick.

on Lancaster and Tudor aircraft; the only jet investigations made up to that time were for the Tudor 8 and the Brabazon 3 projects, with the latter designed for a number around Mach 7.

The original conception of the Delta was not a result of spontaneous inspiration, but was arrived at by, what seemed at the time to be, an honest design study encompassing a whole series of aircraft, some with tails, some tailless, each type checked for a range of aspect ratios and weights. In retrospect, Lindley shuddered to think how much reliance was placed on the wing weight formula used, but the end product seemed to justify the means.

The first preliminary study was made for aircraft of aspect ratios not less than four, and the results clearly showed that the aircraft required would be tailless and would have a much lower aspect ratio – probably about two. A second investigation, covering the lower aspect ratios, gave a solution at 2·4, which was inevitably a Delta wing. Bob knew that Lippisch had been working on a Delta fighter and was able to see some reports on his coal burning, ram jet Delta in Frankfurt during a trip to Germany in 1945, and the possibility of making use of this configuration for a bomber was most intriguing. More elaborate checks were made, but they only served to confirm the Delta configuration.

The design study in the first part of the original issue of the brochure was an elaboration of that used to arrive at the configuration. The basic method of this study was the same as that used originally.

The original arrangement of the aircraft was, of course, somewhat more advanced than that which was finally proposed in the brochure, as it would look advanced even today. It had boundary layer suction combined with a movable cockpit, so that the pilot could have good vision even when the aircraft was at 30° incidence, and it had a very advanced arrangement of combined elevator, air brakes and variable area jet pipe nozzle.

Just about the time these first drawings were finished, Roy Chadwick recovered from his illness. Chadwick was considerably shaken to see the proposal – he had left the project as a sort of jet-propelled Lincoln and returned to find something apparently from a Buck Rogers comic strip in its place. He expressed his doubts very forcibly – Lindley remembers going home and sulking all weekend, as he was very much in love with his project and could not stand the criticism. However, by Monday, Roy Chadwick had decided that it had its good points, and from there on he waded in with great enthusiasm and did much to make it a practical aircraft.

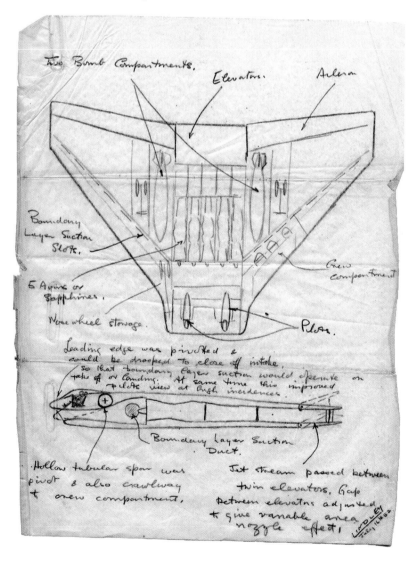

During this period of early development, the aircraft underwent a number of changes. One proposal had five Avon or Sapphire jet engines. In the end, both engines were to power the first prototype Vulcan. In the interests of simplicity, it was decided to go for a twin-engine version, and, for this, it required an engine of around 20,000lb static thrust. Chadwick had written to the aircraft engine industry for proposals for such an engine and the replies were very interesting, ranging from supreme optimism from Armstrong Siddeley to complete pessimism from Metropolitan Vickers. Bob recalls Chadwick taking a $\frac{1}{48}$ scale model of this twin-engine version up to London.

The model was left with Air Marshal Sir John Boothman – Chadwick described how Boothman had 'flown' it around the office, presumably making appropriate noises.

At this stage, the project department heard of the Bristol T.E.1/46 jet engine, which was being designed for the Aircraft Division of Bristol Aeroplane Company; it was to be used in a long-range, high-flying bomber designated Type 172. The general specification of the Type 172 was similar to the Ministry of Supply (MoS) specification that was later responsible for the Vulcan and Victor. The project office at Bristol prepared a brochure that was submitted to the Ministry of Supply in March 1946 and, in July of that year, the T.E.1/46 engine specification was issued.

Later to be named 'Olympus', it was investigated by the Initial Projects Department at Chadderton. A four-engine aircraft was designed using this engine and was adopted for the tender brochure on the Avro Type 698, which was submitted to the MoS in May 1947, just six months from the initial MoS B35/46 requirement.

The other feature that was kicked around considerably was the crew accommodation. The first proposal had the crew compartment inside the wing, with the pilots under two fighter type hoods. Then the requirement for a jettisonable crew compartment was emphasised and much effort was devoted to getting the crew into the minimum nacelle, demountable just aft of the pressure bulkhead. Additionally, a multiple parachute was packed into the fairing aft of the canopy. This design was put forward in the brochure. Unfortunately, this requirement was later dropped due to the considerable research time required to solve the technical problems of having this type of system. In those days, the radar scanner was also installed inside the wing. The first issue of the brochure was finished in April 1947.

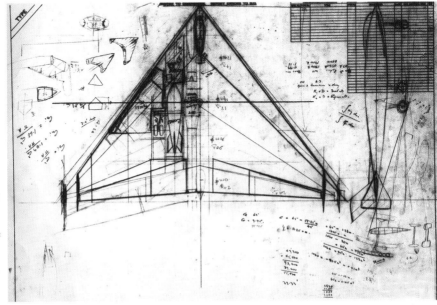

Early ideas made by Roy Chadwick, and workings by Chief Aerodynamicist Eric Priestly, who was succeeded in 1949 by Roy Ewans (later Chief Designer) at Avro in 1955.

Avro's Brief Description to Meet B35/46 Specification

Avro used all the available information, of which they were aware, from British and German Reports in their design study. It was to be propelled by four Jet engines, each of around 9,000lb static thrust capacity, with the engines completely buried in the wing.

The fuel was carried in the leading edge of the wing in ten separate tank compartments, each holding one-tenth of the total fuel capacity. These compartments were fitted with flexible tanks which were removable through access doors in the main spar web.

The crew were to be housed in a nacelle which formed a continuation of the nose of the aerofoil. This nacelle was kept as small as possible, compatible with adequate room for the crew to perform their duties. It was pressurised by means of centrifugal blowers driven off the auxiliary gearboxes.

A fairing behind the pilot's canopy contained the parachutes for supporting the nacelle after it was released from the aircraft, and the doors of this canopy were opened by means of a static line attached to the main aircraft structure and the door release, with a secondary manually operated release inside the nacelle. The engines have been kept very close to the centreline of the aircraft, so that the offset thrust in the case of an engine failure is very small and should be easily controlled.

The speed requirement of 500 knots at heights between 36,000ft and 50,000ft when the speed of sound is 574 knots implies that the critical Mach number must be greater than 0.872.

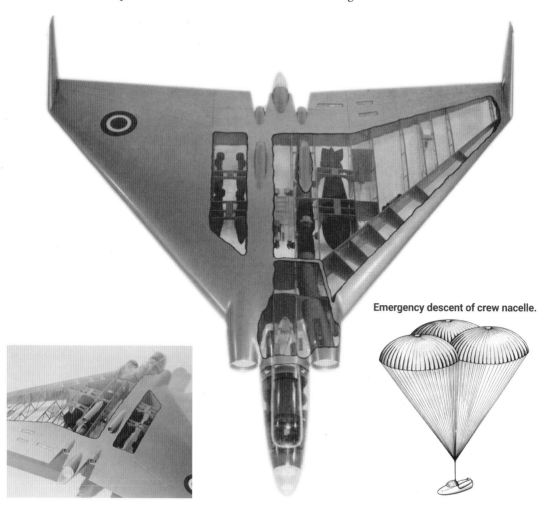

Emergency descent of crew nacelle.

The flying controls were based on those developed for the Armstrong Siddeley AW52 and consisted of an unusual arrangement of double elevons along the wing trailing edge. Boundary layer suction control is provided over the span covered by the elevons.

Dimensions
Wingspan 91ft 6in
Length 92ft 0in
Max Height 16ft 6in

Gross Weight
104,000lb
B35/46 specification

Range
3.350nm

Height
45,000−50,000ft

Speed
500 knots

Total Bomb Load
20,000lb

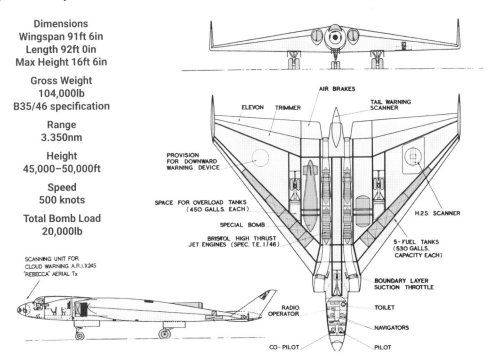

AIR BRAKES

ELEVON   TRIMMER

TAIL WARNING
SCANNER

PROVISION
FOR DOWNWARD
WARNING DEVICE

SPACE FOR OVERLOAD TANKS
(450 GALLS. EACH)

H.2S. SCANNER

SPECIAL BOMB

BRISTOL HIGH THRUST
JET ENGINES (SPEC. T.E. 1/46)

5- FUEL TANKS
(530 GALLS.
CAPACITY EACH)

SCANNING UNIT FOR
CLOUD WARNING A.R.I.X245
'REBECCA' AERIAL Tx

BOUNDARY LAYER
SUCTION THROTTLE

RADIO
OPERATOR

TOILET

NAVIGATORS

CO - PILOT

PILOT

Competition

Most preliminary aircraft design studies were based on research at the Royal Aircraft Establishment at Farnborough, which had the only large-scale, high-speed wind tunnel facility in the UK. Many of these research programmes were based on meeting future military or civil requirements, developed over several years by strategic groups.

The RAE studied design concepts by each competing aircraft manufactures, and these early studies nominally stood an equal chance until all were completed and compared. The overall design of the chosen concept would then be restricted to a very small team of designers, aerodynamicists and stress men who had been security cleared for the projects that were classified 'Secret'. The projects remained secret until the aircraft were finally taken out of service.

At the tender design conference held on 28 July 1947, to discuss the merits of six aircraft companies' submitted tenders, it was decided to proceed with wind tunnel testing of the Avro low aspect ratio Delta wing, and high aspect ratio wings of the Armstrong Whitworth and Handley Page submissions.

Handley Page Type HP90 (Victor)

The Handley Page HP80, later named Victor, was built to the same specification as the Vulcan and was its main direct competitor. The Victor made its first flight on 24 December 1952. It used a crescent wing planform that had a wingspan of 110ft. When the Victor was shown not to be suitable for the low role, it was decided to convert it to an aerial tanker. Twenty-four B2 Victors were converted to the tanker role at Woodford when Handley Page went into liquidation in 1970. Shown above is XL231, used in the development of the Victor K2 refuelling tanker.

Vickers Type 660 (Valiant)

The Vickers Company was issued with tender B9/48 to OR229 on 3 August 1948, which was ostensibly written around the Vickers Type 660, and later became known as the Vickers Valiant. The Type 660 had a lower performance than the Avro Type 698 and Handley Page HP80 but offered the advantage of being available at an earlier date.

The Valiant was the first of the 'V' bombers and the first to enter RAF service. The first prototype, WB210, first flew on 18 May 1951, powered by four Rolls-Royce Avon jet engines. It was officially named 'Valiant' the following month. The Valiant wing had a 'compound sweep' configuration and had a 45-degree angle of sweepback in the inner third of the wing, reducing to an angle of about 24 degrees at the tips, and a wingspan of 114ft 4in. Seen here is the only prototype of the Valiant B2, painted all black at the 1953 Farnborough Air Show.

Royal Aircraft Establishment Initial (RAE) Assessment Phase

Kenneth W Newby recounts his time working as the scientist investigating the high Mach number aerodynamic and performance characteristics of Delta wings at the RAE in Farnborough.

When the RAE became aware that Avro's submission in the contest for a medium-range, high-altitude, high Mach number bomber was to have a Delta configuration, it was realised that, because most Delta research had related to thin wings for supersonic applications, very little was known about the behaviour, aerodynamics, and performance of thicker wings of proposed sweepback, at high subsonic Mach numbers. Without such knowledge, it would be difficult to assess the Avro proposal to the same standard as those from other contenders, which had high aspect ratio wings.

To correct this situation, a model of a Delta wing/body combination, with the fuselage of the proposed aircraft and wing of the same leading-edge sweepback and airfoil section (10 per cent thick laminar flow section with thickness at 40 per cent chord), was designed and manufactured for the RAE High Speed Wind Tunnel.

The sweepback of the Delta wing, varying from leading edge to trailing edge, also presented a problem, as it was becoming apparent from other test data that, although the type of section used by Avro resulted in an increase of critical Mach number on unswept wings, a more forward maximum thickness position was beneficial on swept wings. A second model was made, therefore, having a NACA 0010 wing section (the same thickness/chord ratio, but with maximum thickness at 30 per cent chord) to determine the type of aerofoil most suitable for a Delta wing.

The performance of the wing with the more forward thickness position proved to be superior to that with the section selected by Avro. This data was discussed with Avro who, as a result, changed the section being used in their design to the NACA 0010.

The high Mach number drag results for wings with both sections were disappointing, being significantly worse than those to be expected for an un-tapered swept wing having the same sweepback as that at the maximum thickness/chord line. This was interesting, as there were some indications that less tapered swept wings were not achieving the full benefits of sweepback which had been predicted theoretically.

To study this problem, a larger scale wing/body half model (with a 10 per cent thick NACA 0010 aerofoil section) with pressure plotting provision over the whole wing was built and tested over the whole speed and incidence range.

The force and moment characteristics of this model were similar to those of the corresponding complete model, showing that an increase in Reynold's number (due to the larger model scale) had not improved the results. The pressure plots showed a large loss of effective sweepback over the wing root and tip sections, resulting in the early formation of shock waves in both areas.

At this time, Dr Kuchemann and Dr Weber were studying the flows on untapered swept wings, using linearised theory (as used in the original predictions of the flow over swept wings) and they realised that, on early studies, no account had been taken of the singularities at the root and tip. When they introduced these singularities, they found that there was also a loss of effective sweepback in the root and tip areas of un-tapered wings.

Newby, therefore, started a theoretical study of the effects of thickness and planform taper on the flows over the roots and tips of tapered wings. This work was reported in an RAE Technical Note and later as an American Research Council (ARC) report. The results were also incorporated into a paper on wing design prepared by the Transonic Aerodynamics Committee of the Royal Aeronautical Society, a committee of which Newby was a member for more than a decade and Vice Chairman for two periods of three years, separated by three years as Chairman.

Using these theoretical effects of planform and thickness taper on flows at the wing root, Newby predicted that the maximum thickness/chord ratio increased by 30 per cent (ie increased to 13 per cent). These changes could be achieved by changing to a NACA 0013 aerofoil section at the root and then halving the chord wise percentage ahead of the maximum thickness position and stretching those behind the original 30 per cent chord by 21.4 per cent. This made it easy to connect the new root section to the original NACA 0010 section at a chosen position further out on the wing, by using straight lines between equivalent percentages of the chord wise positions ahead of and behind the maximum thickness positions.

When the potential benefits of this modification were explained to Roy Ewans, Chief Aerodynamicist, and the design team at Avro, they agreed to consider the effects on the wing design, particularly when it was realised that the added thickness at the root might enable the air intakes to be moved from under the wing, to the root leading edge (a position less vulnerable to debris ingestion) without having intake ducts either side of the fuselage, as in some of their studies. Design studies and programme dates suggested that, if the modification could be contained inboard of the existing transport joint, the delay to the programme would be acceptable.

However, it needed a separate presentation by Newby to the Chief Designer before the modification was approved; this was a great risk for Avro to take, as it was not possible to delay the decision until a wind tunnel model could be made and tested.

1948

A vro received a contract for two prototype B.35/46 bombers, VX770 and VX777, dated 22 June 1948. Handley Page received a contract for two prototypes, WB771 and WB775, dated 11 March 1949.

Major Design Changes

Development work in the RAE high-speed wind tunnel at Farnborough had shown a general need for special means to retain adequate control at air speeds somewhat above the critical Mach number. The solution indicated by RAE was the addition of all-moving pointed wing tips and these were applied to the Delta bomber. This addition to the planform caused a considerable aft movement of the required centre of gravity, necessitating a complete redisposition of the equipment. An extra advantage associated with the addition of these pointed wing tips was an increase in aspect ratio from 2.5 to 3.0, which was in line with RAE advice for obtaining a greater height over the target.

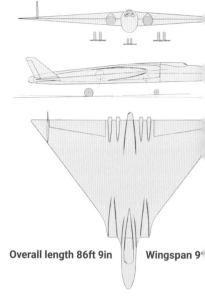

High speed wind tunnel tests showed that two changes in the original wing section were desirable to increase the critical Mach number and to reduce the low-speed profile drag. The first was to reduce the thickness chord ratio from 12 per cent to 10 per cent, and the second was to move forward the chord wise position for maximum thickness from 40 per cent to 30 per cent. With these two alterations, the critical Mach number of the aircraft would attain the value 0.88 for normal cruise.

Following the rearrangement of the engines in line abreast and the thinning of the wing, it was found preferable to use a single bomb bay on the centreline of the aircraft, instead of the two bomb bays shown in the tender brochure. In the single bomb bay, there was space available for a cylindrical special bomb; as no one knew what shape the bomb would be, this represented the most difficult shape of special bomb.

Overall length 86ft 9in   **Wingspan 9**

By September 1948, a new major design landmark was reached; the moveable wing tips had disappeared to make way for a central fin and rudder; the central fin would also provide for an attachment of a tail plane should this prove necessary.

The elevon had been split into elevators and ailerons. Another major change was in the air intake configuration from the large circular 'pitot entry' to a rectangular nose entry. The design was pretty much frozen by then, with work by the RAE enabling final dimensions to be completed. This included the engine intakes and wing leading edge.

Early model showing redesigned rectangular air intake. The moveable wing tips had also been removed and a central fin added.

The general outline had been hardened to allow design to begin, however, it was felt that concern on possible aerodynamic troubles with the configuration did not justify such an immediate commitment. In view of the fact that the first scale model, 707, was scheduled to fly in September 1949, it was felt that final decisions which particularly influenced control layout and design could be deferred for about a year. This programme fitted well within the actual design office commitments at that time.

1949

Third Scale Flying Model

This aircraft was primarily intended to provide data covering the low speed flying and control qualities of Delta aircraft. To this end, the first aircraft was limited to the maximum speed of 300 knots equivalent airspeed (EAS), in order to simplify design problems and accelerate its completion. This aircraft was considerably out of scale as regards the wing body combination.

The issue drawings commenced in June 1948, with the complete aircraft assembled at Woodford in August 1949. After preliminary taxiing trials, it was dismantled and transferred by road to the Aeroplane and Armament Experimental Establishment at Boscombe Down on 26 August 1949.

Type 707 – VX784

The Avro E15/48 was powered by a single Rolls-Royce Derwent 5. It is seen here at Woodford in August 1949. The aircraft utilised many existing components, such as the Avro Athena controls and Hawker P1052 undercarriage, also a Meteor nose wheel and pilot's canopy. It was not fitted with an ejector seat.

On 4 September, Avro Test Pilot Eric Esler took off at 19.50 and, after a 20-minute flight, landed in half light. Short flights continued on the following two days and on 6 September, Esler flew to Farnborough, where it was a static exhibit during the rest of the Society of British Aerospace Companies (SBAC) show. During this period, there had been five flights totalling 2hrs 30mins.

On leaving Farnborough on 30 September, the aircraft crashed near Blackbushe airfield, Hampshire, killing Eric Esler at the early age of 31. A verdict of accidental death was returned at the inquest.

Roy Ewans Joins Avro

Another significant event happened in 1949, when John Roy Ewans was appointed Chief Aerodynamicist to Avro in October 1949. In May 1955, Ewans became Deputy Chief Designer, and later succeeded Stuart Davies as Chief Designer in June 1955.

Ewans was born on 21 December 1917. He completed a post-graduate course in aeronautics that led to an appointment at the RAE in 1938, where for six years he concentrated on aerodynamic research. In 1944, he was a member of a team of investigators sent to France and Germany, and in 1946, he joined the Blackburn Aircraft Company as head of the aerodynamics section of the design office.

By 1960, Roy Ewans was Chief Designer at Avro and is seen here with one of his projects, the Avro 748 turboprop airliner.

1950

The angle of sweep at wing root intakes had changed when it became apparent to the RAE that a compressibility drag rise would take place at a lower Mach number, as Ken Newby at the RAE had suggested, resulting in degradation in performance to unacceptable levels, unless the sweepback at the centre section could be increased over the then design value.

This led to the redesign of the wing root by displacing the line of maximum thickness of the centre part of the wing, near the air intake, forward some 15 per cent of the root chord; this led to scrapping of the complete lines of the wing and all the structure detail that had been schemed. This decision was made at the end of 1949, the first issue of the basic dimensions went to the works in February 1950 and detailed drawings were produced in May 1950. This was to lead to a three-month delay in issuing new drawings.

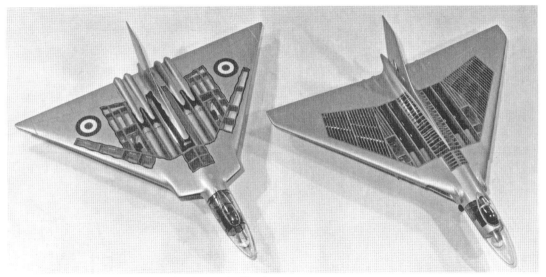

The difference in wing root can be clearly seen in this picture.

Second Third Scale Flying Model

Following the loss of the first Type 707, a second experimental Type 707B was manufactured as a replacement, a new nose and ejector seat were fitted, and airbrakes were fitted to the top of the wing. This aircraft was resonance tested and completed in January 1950.

Roland Falk Joins Avro

Roland 'Roly' John Falk joined Avro in 1950 and took over the test flying of the 707s from the late Eric Esler. After a distinguished flying career, he became Chief Test Pilot at RAE Farnborough in 1943, where he flew jet and rocket-propelled prototypes, including captured German aircraft. In 1946, he became Chief Experimental Test Pilot for Vickers Armstrong.

In 1951, Falk married Leysa Hanson, the daughter of Avro's Chief Test Pilot, Bill Thorn, who was tragically killed alongside Roy Chadwick in the Tudor crash in 1947. On 1 March 1954, Falk was promoted to the unique position of Superintendent of Flying.

Type 707B – VX790

Left: Avro Type 707B pictured on 2 November 1950 on one of VX790's many proving flights.

Below: Avro Type 707B VX790 first flew on 6 September 1950 from Boscombe Down by Avro Test Pilot Roly Falk.

1951

On 21 March 1951, engine surging became apparent at 33,000ft and above around 14,300rpm. This led to a change of engine on 3 May 1951, with a modified Derwent V engine selected. A flight test report on air intake efficiencies was sent to Mr Ewans, and a design sketch was supplied by him for the report; this led to a modification of the air intake on VX790. On 26 January 1956, the aircraft went to the Empire Test Flying School (ETPS) for test pilot training. On 25 September 1956, it suffered a landing accident and went into storage. It was later used for spares at RAF Bedford.

Type 707A – WD280

In regard to air intake, the Type 707A was more representative of the Type 698, although the relatively large fuselage would alter conditions inboard of the wing. The 707A was mainly used to test the high-speed envelope and confirmed that buffeting at high Mach numbers would be a problem, as suggested at the RAE during early wind tunnel tests that at the time were not reported to Avro.

On 23 May 1951, Avro 707A WD280 arrived at Boscombe Down to be assembled. Fitting of the components started on 24 May, and, by 28 May, the wings had been attached. The first flight of was on 14 June 1951, 11 months after the Type 707B. The air intake was more representative of the Type 698.

1952

First Prototype Build at Chadderton

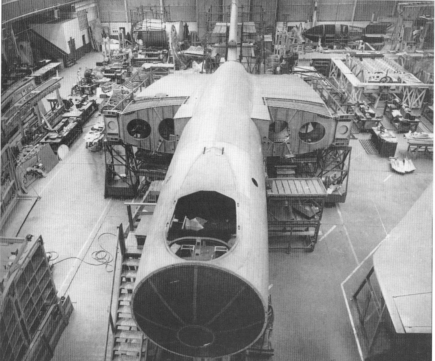

Above: In the background, a wooden mock-up of the Type 698 can be seen.

Left: By 1952, construction of the Type 698 was well advanced in the Experimental Bay at Chadderton. A mock-up of the proposed bomb casing can be seen in the background.

Above left: Prototype wing under construction at Chadderton.

Above right: Sections were transported by road to Woodford. Pictured is the main centre section.

Above: On the way to be painted, August 1952.

Below: A freshly painted first prototype on 22 August 1952. In the background, the Avro Shackleton can be seen.

In the foreground is the Avro Type 707A.

Resonance set-up at Woodford flight sheds,
25 July 1952.

First prototype being assembled at Woodford Flight Sheds on 24 July 1952.

Hangar No 5 at Woodford flight sheds, 24 July 1952.

Avro Management examining the Type 698 on 22 August 1952.

Above: The first prototype, pictured on 29 August 1952.

Below: Type 698, pictured the day before the first flight on 29 August 1952. It is seen here prior to its engine test.

First Flight, 30 August 1952

The first flight began on 30 August 1952 at 09.45 and took off from the Poynton end of the runway. The prototype flew to a height of 10,000ft and landed back at Woodford 35 minutes later in the capable hands of Roly Falk.

The flight was not without incident; the main undercarriage door fairing attachments detached from the aircraft and had to be inspected before landing back at Woodford. At the time, the Type 698 was only equipped for one pilot to fly and had no cockpit pressurisation or wing fuel system. As an interim measure, the Type 698 was powered by four Rolls-Royce Avon jet engines of 6,500lb thrust.

Above left: **Roly Falk in his flying suit.**

Above right: **Roly Falk taxiing the Type 698 on the way to its first flight at Woodford.**

Above left: **Fast taxi.**

Above right: **Take-off sequence.**

Above and below: **These pictures were taken by Avro's Chief Inspector, A C 'Sandy' Jack.**

Landing Back at Woodford

Landing back at Woodford, minus rear main undercarriage door fairings that became detached during the flight.

Examining the main undercarriage after the first flight, which lasted more than 30 minutes.

Top Management Team

Prime movers in the design and production of the Type 698. Pictured from left to right; Mr J A R 'Jimmy' Kay (Director), Wg Cdr R 'Roly' Falk (Test Pilot), Sir William Farren (Technical Director), Mr S D 'Stuart' Davies (Chief Designer), Sir Roy Dobson (Managing Director), Gilbert Whitehead (Project Designer), and C E 'Teddy' Fielding (Production Director) in front of the first prototype Vulcan.

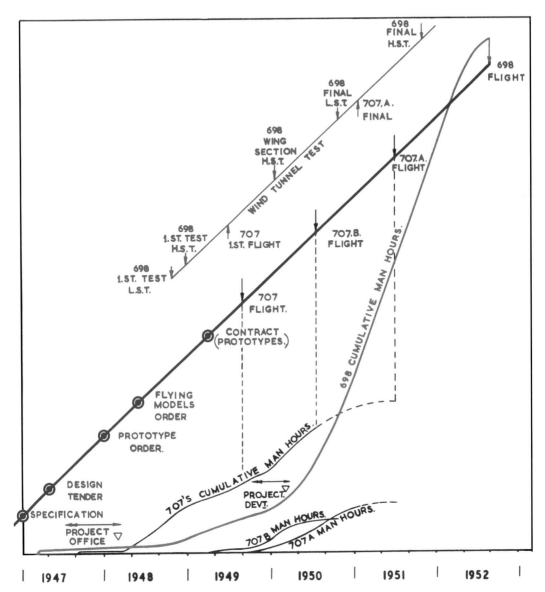

The actual time from issue of the first manufacturing drawings to the works to the first flight of the first prototype was 23 months; this was due to the unconventional configuration which was responsible for at least half the total time in the design of the first prototype.

To summarise this part of the development of the Type 698, it is interesting to note how much effort was made by the workforce to achieve its first flight. Between 1947 and the first flight of the 698 in 1952, Avro was involved in the design and manufacture of a variety of aircraft; these included the production of 466 Ansons with the last 24 being delivered in 1952. They also produced 86 Shackletons, five Ashtons, 22 Athenas, five Lancastrians, 28 Tudors, 20 Yorks and three Type 707 Delta research aircraft during that period.

This output put enormous pressure on the design and production departments and the skills and talent employed by Avro at that time. The design and production of the 698 was a huge risk taken by all those concerned, with a lot of reputations at stake. The fact that the 698 became the spearhead of bomber command, and their biggest threat during the Cold War, is a great testament to those pioneering achievements.

First Public Appearance

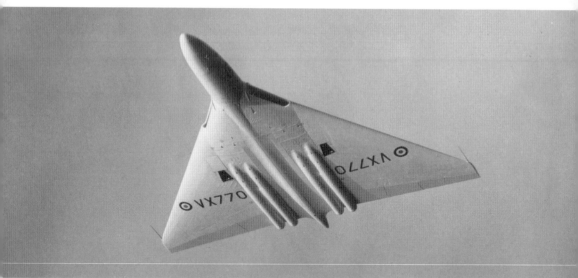

The above picture shows VX770 before its appearance at the SBAC show in September 1952; it was part of a series of pictures taken for publicity purposes. The aircraft was minus its main undercarriage door fairings and, due to the fact that it would be flying the few hours of its life under speed limitations, it was decided to carry on flying without these fairings. Some pictures published by Avro were retouched to show the fairings in place.

Left: Yet to be named Vulcan, the Type 698 is seen here with the red 707A WD280, flown by Jimmy Nelson. The Blue Avro 707B not pictured here was flown by Avro Test Pilot Jack Wales.

Below: This air-to-air picture was taken on 8 September 1952.

When the Type 698 made its first public appearance at the SBAC Air Show at Farnborough in September 1952, the black anti dazzle panel under the cockpit window had disappeared. The aircraft was based at Boscombe Down during its appearance at the Show. The 698 was described as being one of the most photogenic machines ever to take to the air.

Vulcan Name Adopted for the Avro Type 698

Sir John Slessor, Chief of the Air Staff (CAS), ruled that the Avro Type 698 would have a name beginning with 'V' to follow the Vickers Valiant. The name Vulcan was revealed to the public during the week ending 24 October 1952. Sir John Slessor was a major proponent of Britain developing a nuclear deterrent force, and retired from the RAF in 1952.

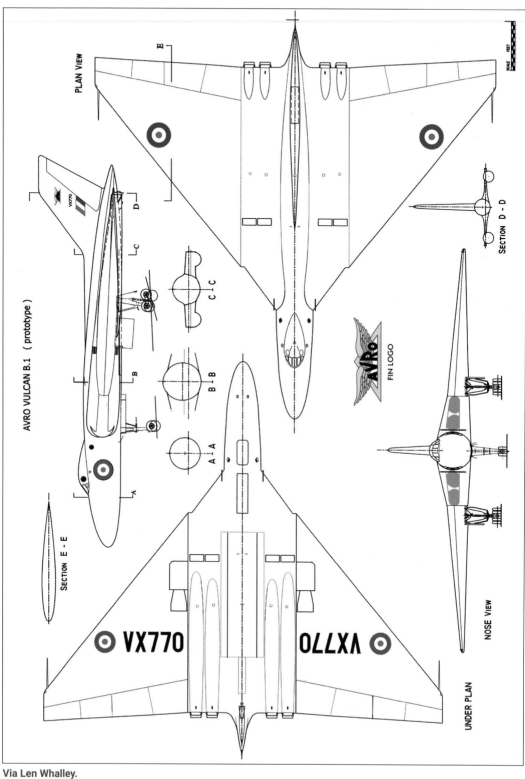

PLAN VIEW

SCALE FEET

SECTION D - D

AVRO VULCAN B.1 (prototype)

C - C

B - B

A - A

AVRO
FIN LOGO

SECTION E - E

VX770

VX770

NOSE VIEW

UNDER PLAN

Via Len Whalley.

1953

Avro Type 707A – WZ736

Avro Type 707A WZ736 at a Woodford Family Day, along with its big brother. The first 707A had turned out to be such a useful and reliable aircraft that the RAE had a wish for one for its own purposes, and a second 707A was built to contract 6/acft/7470/CB.(6), dated 13 November 1951. It was part of a contract that also included the duo powered 707C aircraft. After WZ736 had been assembled at the Avro facility at Bracebridge Heath, Avro Test Pilot Jimmy Nelson flew WZ736 from RAF Waddington on 20 February 1953. The aircraft was saved for public display.

Avro Twin Seat Type 707C – WZ744

The Avro Type 707C was a two-seat Delta wing aircraft, powered by one Rolls-Royce Derwent 8 turbine engine and designed for research and familiarisation of pilots with characteristics of tailless aircraft of Delta planform.

Two Type 707C aircraft were allocated serial numbers in 1952; the first, WZ739, was never built. The second, WZ744, was flown for the first time on 1 July 1953 from RAF Waddington, with Sqn Ldr Jack Wales at the controls. The aircraft joined the RAE in January 1956 and made a substantial research contribution into the development of fly-by-wire controls. The aircraft flew with the RAE until September 1966 and was selected to be saved to be put on display at the RAF museum at Cosford, near Wolverhampton.

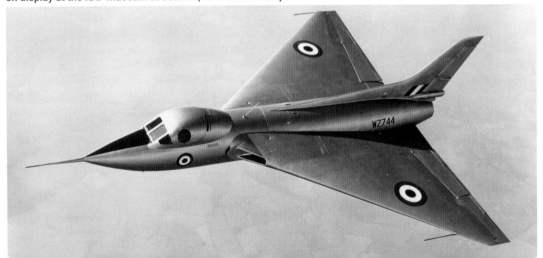

Sapphire Engine Vulcan

During one of VX770's high altitude test flights in February 1953, Roly Falk was extending the airbrakes when the port outer airbrake under the wing fractured. With the aircraft grounded, it was decided to take the opportunity to change the engines to the more powerful Armstrong Siddeley Sapphire Sa6 of 8000lb static thrust. A full wing fuel system had also been fitted. By June 1953, the first prototype, now fitted with the Sapphire engines, flew with Roly Falk at the controls to test the new fuel system up to 30,000ft.

The Vulcan was highly manoeuvrable for an aircraft of its size, especially at high altitude, where it could out manoeuvre most fighters at that time.

Second Prototype Vulcan

The second prototype was powered by four Olympus 100 engines, although these were later changed to the more powerful Olympus 101 engines following a heavy landing at Farnborough in July 1954. As with VX770, it was just in time to make its first public appearance with the first prototype Vulcan at the memorable 1953 SBAC Show.

Above left and above right: Take-off and landing of the initial first flight of the second prototype Vulcan on 3 September 1953, with Roly Falk at the controls. The second prototype was powered by the Olympus 100 engine.

A Date to Remember at the 1953 SBAC Farnborough Air Show

Above left: Flight magazine cover, celebrating the 1953 Farnborough Air Show.

Above: All three Avro Type 707 small Delta aircraft were on display in the static park at the 1953 Farnborough Air Show.

Below: Delta formation taken on 11 September 1953.

Early picture of the first prototype VX770, showing its elegant lines.

Air-to-air pictures of VX770; a distinguishing feature was the lack of bomb blister, which was not specified for the first prototype. Also note the single pitot on the nose. These two pictures were taken on 29 September 1953, from the rear of a USAF Fairchild C-119 Packet.

1954

Prototype Development

By December 1954, the first prototype had completed 27 take-offs and landings, and 21hrs 5mins in the air.

It is interesting to note that the Handley Page Victor, which was built to the same B35/46 specification as the Vulcan and was its main competitor, made its first flight on 24 December 1952, nearly three months after the Vulcan. Like the Vulcan, in April 1953, the Victor was powered by four Armstrong Siddeley Sapphire (Sa.6) engines.

The first prototype Vulcan was a very basic aircraft at the time, which was more or less suggested in the September 1948 report, in order to speed up the testing programme.

Second prototype, VX777, takes off from Woodford on 31 March 1954.

By April 1953, the first prototype VX770 had four Armstrong Siddeley Sapphire (Sa.6) engines installed, the wing fuel system was fully operative, and the cockpit pressurisation was also made operative. It also included an intensive flight programme, which included demonstrations. By this time, 62 flights had been completed. The flight tests covered an extensive field, engine handling and installation tests, fuel tests, trim curves, strain gauge tests on wing and structure and air brakes. Position error tests and drag measurements were also carried out.

During this period, the second prototype Vulcan, VX777, was fitted with Bristol Olympus 100 engines and made its initial flight on 3 September 1953. The aircraft immediately thereafter had a number of engineering changes, including modifications to the Olympus engine control systems. Additional systems were also completed, the object being to carry out handling trials at the highest possible altitude.

The first prototype during this period was carrying out extensive handling tests. The tests included trim changes, due to airbrakes both at high Mach numbers and in landing configuration. Manoeuvring stability, trim points, handling tests with engines stopped and with power controls switched off, were also carried out.

On 27 July 1954, VX777 was damaged during a heavy landing at Farnborough. During the subsequent repair work, Olympus 101 engines were installed. Also, as the preliminary results from the structural test specimen were becoming available, a number of strengthening modifications were incorporated.

Disaster was averted thanks to the flying skills of Roland Falk when the rudder jammed during a flight test with Farnborough personnel. This resulted in the second prototype VX777 making a heavy landing at Farnborough on 27 July 1954. At the time, it was fitted with Olympus 100 engines of 9,500lb thrust; the aircraft was soon repaired, and more powerful Olympus 101 engines rated at 10,000lb thrust were fitted. The aircraft was subsequently used for a preliminary assessment of the Vulcan by the Aeroplane and Armament Experimental Establishment (A&AEE) in May 1955.

Boundary Layer Experiments

It became apparent that, during high altitudes and speeds on the early test flights with the 707A and VX777, the wing was suffering from buffet problems and affecting the performance. In the summer of 1954, new Test Pilot Jimmy Harrison had flown WD280 trying wing fences, vortex generators and notches to help find a solution to the boundary layer problem.

The RAE at Farnborough, in the meantime, proposed the fitting of a kink leading edge, and an experimental mock version of the leading edge extension was tested on WD280, using a technique of applied 'g' to simulate the correct Vulcan Mach No CL relationships. The wind tunnel prediction was confirmed by flights in early 1955 and modification to the B.Mk1 Vulcan was authorised.

On 21 March 1955, discussions with the Australian Aeronautical Research Council were held at A V Roe between senior officials of both governments, which included discussions about obtaining a 707. By this time, WD280 had completed its intensive test programme on the new wing planform destined for the Vulcan. By November 1955, it was decided to provide WD280 for further research into low-speed handling of a Delta wing aircraft in Australia.

Above left: Jimmy G Harrison joined Avro in February 1954 and became Chief Test Pilot in 1958. In 1968, he was awarded the OBE for his role in the development of the Vulcan.

Above right: Early boundary layer wing fence experiments on VX790. Due to undesirable wing buzz caused by airflow over the wing tips large wing fences were fitted. It was not enough to solve the problem and led to the redesign of the outer wing leading edge.

Below: Avro Type 707A WD280 with kink wing leading edge.

1955

Production Well Underway at Chadderton and Woodford

Nose build at Chadderton.

Chadderton production line.

Above left: Scaffolding around the wing jig at Woodford, 8 December 1954.

Above right: Structural test rig at Woodford, 27 January 1955. In 1954, the third Vulcan B.Mk1 of the Avro production line was subjected to a comprehensive series of structural tests. Two years later, these tests were passed with complete success.

Below: Second production aircraft XA890, pictured in new assembly at Woodford in 1955.

First Production Aircraft

The initial flight of the first production Vulcan B.Mk1 aircraft was on 4 February 1955. Initially, Bristol Olympus 100 engines were fitted with the wing planform identical to that of the first prototype aircraft. On 18 and 19 June 1955, XA889 made a flypast at the Paris Air Show.

During October 1955, XA889 was grounded to enable the wing leading edge modification to be incorporated and auto-stabilisation system fitted. Flight testing recommenced in mid-February 1956. After a series of check flights, the aircraft was fitted with Olympus 101 engines and delivered to the A&AEE to begin its official trials on 15 March 1956 for the official Certificate of Airworthiness (CofA) release of the Vulcan B.Mk1. The release was issued by the Ministry of Supply on 29 May 1956.

At the 1955 Farnborough Air Show, Roly Falk demonstrated the manoeuvrability of the Vulcan when he slow rolled the second B.Mk1, XA890, immediately after take-off. Later, at the Farnborough Air Show, the Vulcan showed the 'toss bomb' technique by rolling out at the top of the climb.

The above picture shows the first production B.Mk1, XA889, taking off on its first flight on 4 February 1955.

Air-to-air picture of XA889 taken on its first flight; early production Vulcans still had a straight wing before being retro fitted with the new kink wing.

The picture above shows the third production Vulcan, XA891, on 4 October 1955, with its original straight wing.

This famous picture shows XA891 flying over Mersey Estuary with its new kink wing. It first flew on 22 September 1955, with Avro Test Pilot Johnny Baker at the controls. On 31 January 1957, it went to A V Roe at Langar in preparation for the B.O1.6 Olympus series 200 trials. By then, it had the new kink wing fitted.

New Wing for Vulcan B.Mk1

Ken Newby remembers that early flow visualisation checks done by the RAE at Farnborough showed no obvious signs of shock waves over the inner regions of the wing, but there were, as might be expected, still signs of problems over the outboard sections of the wing.

The outer wing modifications suggestions were not communicated to Avro at this time, as the prototype design had been frozen, and production of the prototype was under way. Once the modified Avro 707A and the prototype VX777 were flying and into the performance programme, one would be able to judge whether there was any need for further modification, without having to make judgements about scale effects (though these were not expected to be very significant with this type of pressure distribution).

No reports of problems were received as the flight tests progressed for what seemed a long time, and the manufacture of the first batch of production aircraft had been approved before the flight envelope was expanded enough to cover the full operational load, altitude, and speed. Above a lift coefficient of about 0.2 at the cruising speed, flow separation, presumably over the outer wing, was reported to be causing buffeting, much as had been indicated by the tunnel tests.

First flight of the second prototype, VX777, with the new Phase 2 wing, was on 4 October 1955. It is seen here taking off from Woodford on 10 October 1955.

Newby was thankful that the long analysis of the flows over the outer wing had already been undertaken, and that he was able to present his suggestions to Avro quite quickly. Some consternation was caused when the implications of the modifications were realised. It meant a redesign of the outer half of the wing and, unless an intermediate modification could be incorporated retrospectively on existing aircraft, the scrapping of wings already coming off the production line. An interim modification would have to be limited to the area ahead of the front spar.

After further study of the pressure distributions, Newby proposed a simple, thin, drooped extension, which was faired into the upper surface of the original leading edge, and with a small arc fairing the lower surface junction between the extension and original leading edge. The drooped leading edge extended the section ahead of the front spar by about 100 per cent at the 75 per cent span position. The 'Newby Droop' succeeded in enabling the B.Mk1 aircraft to just achieve its design requirements when retrofitted with this droop.

Once again, he had to explain his thinking to Avro's higher management. This time it was to Sir William 'Bill' Farren, whom he had known when he was Director of the RAE. He asked the National Physical Laboratory (NPL) to carry out two dimensional tests on the section as part of a series which Dr Robbin Lock was supervising and which substantiated Newby's assumptions.

With the proposed fitting of a kink leading edge by the RAE, an experimental mock-version of the leading edge extension was tested on WD280, using a technique of applied 'g' to simulate the correct Vulcan Mach Number CL relationships. The wind tunnel prediction was confirmed by flights in early 1955, and modification to the B.Mk1 Vulcan was authorised.

Vulcan B.Mk1 Phase 2 Wing

The new Phase 2 wing started on the ninth production aircraft and the rest were retrofitted to most of the first eight aircraft. Production halted whilst the leading edge envelope jig was scrapped and 16 sets of the straight wing leading edge were modified to the new version.

Also shown in the diagram are the positions of the 16 vortex generators used on each Phase 2 wing. These were not used on the larger and thinner B.Mk2 Phase 2C wing.

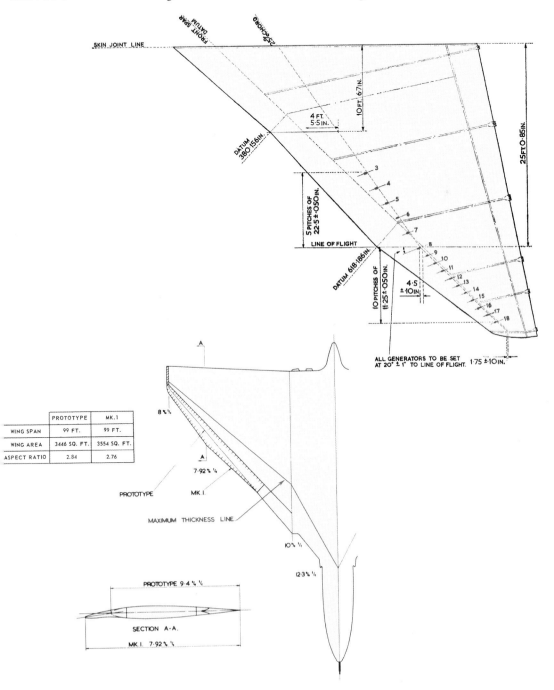

	PROTOTYPE	MK.1
WING SPAN	99 FT.	99 FT.
WING AREA	3446 SQ. FT.	3554 SQ. FT.
ASPECT RATIO	2.84	2.76

1956

The initial CA release on 29 May 1956 enabled the RAF to commence essential flight and ground-crew training that was important to develop the Vulcan B.Mk1 into an effective weapon system as quickly as possible. A number of early production aircraft were therefore used for these tasks.

The new kink wing on XA889 shown being flown from Boscombe Down on 25 March 1956 by Roly Falk during its official trials for CA release. Flight trials on the 707A, and the earlier tests on the prototype Vulcan, had indicated the need to incorporate auto-stabilisation systems. These systems (yaw damper, pitch damper and Mach trimmer) had been designed especially for the Vulcan and were fitted to the VX777 in November 1955. The flight development of these systems was the major task for the second prototype between November 1955 and June 1956. This work took just over 100 hours flying in around 70 flights.

Vulcan line at Woodford on 19 August 1956. Pictured are XA898, XA893, XA892, XA891, XA889 and XA894.

Vulcan BMk.1 Enters RAF Service

When Roly Falk made a night arrival at Boscombe Down in the first production Vulcan, a series of acceptance trials began with A&AEE test pilots of (B) Squadron. At the time of the initial trials, the first Vulcan station at Waddington was being manned in readiness for the delivery of production aircraft.

The officers, NCOs and airmen were near the end of intensive courses of instruction, some of which were conducted in the Avro Technical Training School at Woodford. These trials were completed in May 1956 and the Vulcan was ready to go into service.

The first operational unit was No 83 Squadron, along with No 230 Operational Conversion Unit (OCU), with both being based at RAF Waddington.

The above colour picture shows XA895 in its silver colour scheme. Later, B.Mk1 aircraft were painted in overall anti-flash white to help avoid the effects of a nuclear blast at high level. XA895 first flew from Woodford on 12 August 1956 and was delivered to 230 OCU on 16 August 1956. On 5 March 1958, XA895 returned to Woodford for ECM TI and flight trials. In 1965, the aircraft then went to RRE (Royal Radar Establishment) Pershore for development and trials of Red Steer Mk2. It was later sold for scrap to Bradbury Ltd on 19 September 1968.

Early production Vulcan B.Mk1 being prepared for flight test, pictured at Woodford.

XA891 takes off at Woodford, 18 August 1956.

Avro Type 707 WD280 Goes to Australia

Pictured above WD280 at Woodford on 8 March 1956, prior to going to Australia.

After WD280 had completed an intensive test programme on a new wing planform destined for the Vulcan, by November 1955 it was decided to provide WD280 for further research into the low-speed handling of a Delta wing aircraft. After a complete overhaul, it departed Woodford on 8 March 1956 for Renfrew Airport in Scotland and was loaded on board HMAS *Melbourne* on 9 March 1956. The aircraft had completed a total of 283hrs 10mins flying time.

Tragic End to a Triumphant Overseas Tour of Australia

On 1 October 1956, after a successful tour of Australia, XA897 returned to the United Kingdom when, in low visibility, the aircraft hit the ground short of the Heathrow Airport threshold and in the attempted overshoot, the aircraft banked slowly to starboard then dived into the ground. The pilots, Sqn Ldr Howard, at the controls, and Harry Broadhurst, in the second pilot's seat, ejected from the aircraft and both survived the crash. Freddie Bassett, Avro's technical representative,

perished along with squadron leaders A E Gamble, J A W Stroud and E J James, who, without ejection seats, were unable to escape.

XA897 comes in to land at Avalon airfield in Australia. By this time, the underside airbrakes had changed to a single unit.

1957

Vulcan and Valiant aerial formation at the 1957 Farnborough Air Show. Shown above are XA907, which was delivered to No 83 squadron 12 August 1957, and XA902 from No 230 OCU at Waddington. The Valiant was to become a familiar site at Woodford, as five were allocated for Blue Steel missile development. With the increased high-altitude performance of the Vulcan, crews were fitted with equipment suitable for these attitudes.

Auto Pilot, Military Flight System (MFS) and Auto Landing System Development

VULCAN XA 899
THE FIRST FOUR-JET AIRCRAFT IN THE WORLD TO BE LANDED FULLY AUTOMATICALLY.
R.A.E. BEDFORD
22 ND DECEMBER 1959

Initially, blind landing trials were carried out at Martlesham Heath by the Blind Landing Experimental Unit (BLEU). The unit was formed after experimental work at the Telecommunications Research Establishment (TRE) at Defford in 1945. It later moved to Bedford, where they tested the auto throttle system on the Avro Type 707A required for this method of landing.

At the time, Vulcan B.Mk1 XA899 was developing the Smiths Military Flight System, which was a military development of the system used by commercial airlines. Along with the MFS system, XA899 was flight testing the auto throttle system, which Tony Blackman first trialled in October 1957.

After XH533 had completed its initial B.Mk2 clearance trials at Boscombe Down in June 1959, it returned to Woodford for fitment of a complete automatic landing system. These trials were made at Bedford and the first automatic landing with XH533 was made on 31 August 1961.

The official clearance trials for the Mk10B Autopilot, Military Flight System MFS Mk1B and auto landing system began in May 1963 on XH533, and were tested at Boscombe Down and Bedford. The last flight of XH533 using this feature was on 27 June 1967, with more than 90 successful automatic landings being made at Bedford. The first fully certificated automatic landing system was used on the DH Trident airliner; it confirmed that a leader cable was unnecessary for automatic systems as used by the Vulcan trials aircraft.

Tony Blackman joined Avro as a test pilot in August 1956 and previously worked at Boscombe Down (B) Squadron which was responsible for the evaluation of bomber aircraft. It was here that Blackman was involved in some of the earliest handling assessments of the Vulcan. He became Chief Test Pilot (callsign Avro One) in 1970.

Avro Vulcan B.Mk2

In August 1955, the Vulcan B.Mk2 version was proposed and wing leading edge modification designed. The 'Phase 2C' wing, as it was known, was allotted to be fitted to VX777 and a contract was issued for an aerodynamic prototype on 10 July 1956. The first flight of VX777 with the new 'Phase 2C' wing was made on 31 August 1957.

An early brochure, issued in March 1956, described the aircraft as a high-altitude, long-range bomber powered by four Olympus B.01.6 jet engines of 16,000 or 16,500lb each; depending on which engines were installed, also quoted were four Rolls-Royce Conway stage 3 engines at 16,500lb at sea level static thrust. Cruising altitude was quoted as being 45,000–65,000ft, with a cruising speed of 500 knots. Range with a normal 10,000lb load or 13,000lb special store was 5,000–5,500nm.

Note the drooped leading edge.

The wingspan was increased to 110ft and a new AC electrical system fitted. Another major change was made to the flying controls from elevators and ailerons. These were in the form of four elevons split outboard and inboard on each wing. The term elevon was a combination of elevator and aileron. The rear ECM kit fitted to later B.Mk1A aircraft was also added.

An artificial stability system was included in the form of a pitch damper system, at altitude more than 20,000ft. An auto-mach-trim system was introduced to counteract the tendency towards instability and designed to leave the pilot with the impression of an aircraft with positive static stability throughout. The natural stability of the aircraft in yaw was supplemented by the introduction of a yaw damping system to fulfil the stringent requirements of various roles.

The first public appearance of the B.Mk2 was at the 1957 Farnborough Air Show. This picture was taken in the week before the Farnborough Air Show and shows the Phase 2C wing to best advantage.

Comparison of the B.Mk1 Phase 2 and B.Mk2 Phase 2C wing

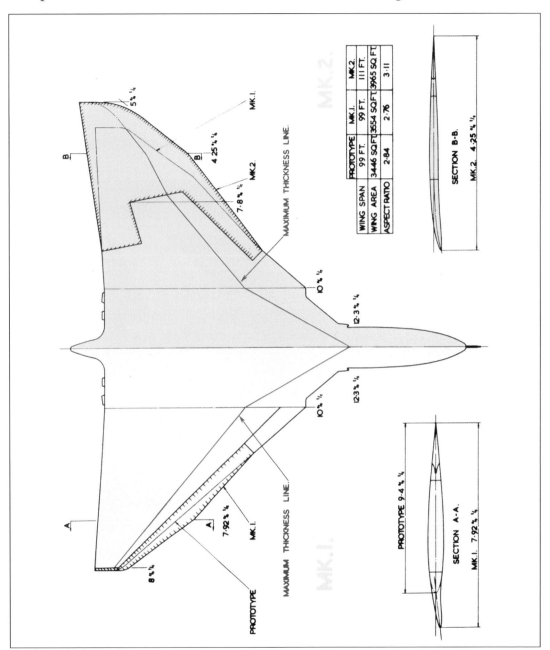

	PROTOTYPE	MK.I.	MK.2.
WING SPAN	99 FT.	99 FT.	111 FT.
WING AREA	3446 SQ FT	3554 SQ FT	3965 SQ FT
ASPECT RATIO	2·84	2·76	3·11

Major Design Changes Introduced in the Vulcan B.Mk2

A. More powerful engines Olympus B.Ol.6. **B**. New outer wing and leading edge. **C**. Elevators and ailerons of the Mk.1 changed to elevons. **D**. New and enlarged rear fuselage to accommodate additional equipment. **E**. AC electrical system. **F**. Rover auxiliary power unit. **G**. Strengthened main and nose undercarriage. **H**. Larger air intake for the future Olympus jet engines eg B.01.21, with around 20,000lb of sea level static thrust.

1958

B.Mk1 Vulcan Enters Service with the Royal Air Force

The first operational unit was No 83 Squadron along with No 230 OCU, with both being based at RAF Waddington. Another squadron, reformed on 1 May 1958 to operate the Vulcan, was the famous No 617 Squadron based at RAF Scampton. The squadron received its first Avro Vulcan aircraft, XH482, on 6 May 1958.

XA900's first flight was on 16 February 1957 and it entered service with No 230 OCU on 25 March 1957; it joined No 101 Squadron at RAF Waddington on 22 June 1960. After being retired from RAF service, XA900 was allocated to the RAF museum at Cosford and was the last B.Mk1 to be scrapped in 1986. It is seen here pictured on 22 August 1958.

Vulcan B.Mk1 XH504 first flew on 30 November 1958. It was later converted to B.Mk1A standard and delivered to RAF Waddington on 8 February 1962.

Rolls-Royce Conway Development

As an alternative power plant to the Bristol Olympus, it was proposed that the Rolls-Royce Conway bypass engine, which had a similar power rating to the Olympus, could be employed. This led to the first prototype being converted to carry the Rolls-Royce Conway at the Avro Langar facility, near Nottingham.

The first prototype, VX770, made its initial flight with four Rolls-Royce Conway RCo.5 engines on 9 August 1957 and was flown to Woodford by Jimmy Harrison for handling tests. On 24 August 1957, the aircraft was delivered to the Rolls-Royce test facility at Hucknall, near Nottingham, for development flying. When VX770 appeared at the 1957 and 1958 SBAC Farnborough Air Show, it

Stripped down XA902 on 19 May 1958.

was crewed by Rolls-Royce personnel, but, on 20 September 1958, it tragically crashed at RAF Syerston during the Battle of Britain display due to structural failure after being overstressed.

With the loss of VX770, Rolls-Royce needed to continue the development of the Conway jet engine and XA902 was chosen for this purpose. The aircraft had a landing accident at RAF Waddington and returned to Woodford by road for repair where it was fitted with Rolls-Royce RCo.11 engines. When all the required modifications were also carried out, which had included a completely new nose section from Chadderton, it was flown to the Rolls-Royce Hucknall airfield on 17 July 1959. It later went on to test the Rolls-Royce Spey low-bypass turbofan engine.

Rolls-Royce made a strong bid to put the Conway into the B.Mk2 Vulcan; they argued that it would achieve commonality with the Victor B2 and widen its sale to airlines.

B.Mk2 First Production Development Aircraft

The first production B.Mk2, XH533, made its first flight on 30 August 1958. It was used for handling, performance and automatic landing trials. It was minus the enlarged rear fuselage used for countermeasures equipment.

1959

This well-known picture, taken on 13 June 1959, shows Vulcan B.Mk1 aircraft XH476, XH475 and XA909 from No 101 Squadron based at Waddington. The aircraft were now painted in the overall white anti-flash paint scheme.

Fire at Chadderton

There was fire damage to Vulcan centre sections at Chadderton Bay One in October 1959; production resumed after a six-week delay. Unfortunately, the majority of company historic records and photographs were destroyed in the fire. Most of the company's photographic negatives were actually spoiled by water and, owing to the company's insurance claim, had to be destroyed without being restored.

B.Mk1 Blue Danube & Yellow Sun installation with ECM equipment

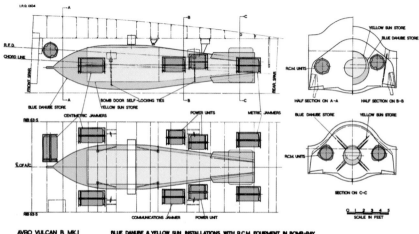

XA891 Incident

On 24 August 1959, the third production Vulcan B.Mk1, XA891, was on a routine test flight from Woodford, with Avro Test Pilot Jimmy Harrison at the controls, when it crashed due to total electrical failure. The aircraft was a development aircraft for the Olympus B.01.6/35 engines. Up to Flight 95, the port two engines had AC alternators with Sundstrand drive units. For Flight 95 to 100, a production Mk 200 engine was fitted in the port inner position, with two B.01.6/3 engines starboard. These were fitted with DC generators for aircraft services. The engine air intakes were altered aft of the front spar to curve the airflow up into the new engine, the front of which were raised 5° above the Olympus 101 datum to accommodate the alternators.

On board from Avro were First Pilot Jimmy Harrison, Second Pilot R G 'Dickie' Proudlove, Radio Operator R S 'Bob' Pogson, Flight Test Observer E H 'Ted' Hartley, and from Bristol Siddeley Engines Ltd, Phil Christie. As the Vulcan got into trouble, Harrison called to abandon the aircraft, with the three rear crew being the first to leave. The two pilots managed to use their ejection seats, but all had difficulty because they were wearing full pressure gear.

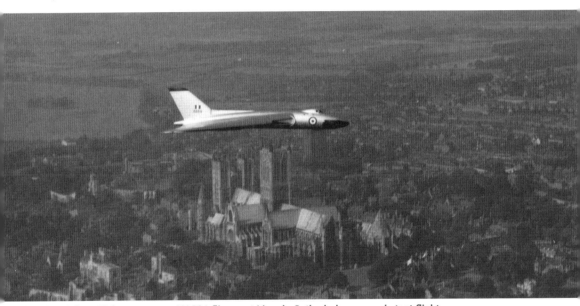

A familiar sight to Vulcan crews as XA891 flies past Lincoln Cathedral on an early test flight.

The remains of XA891 in a field at High Hunsley, Cottingham, Humberside.

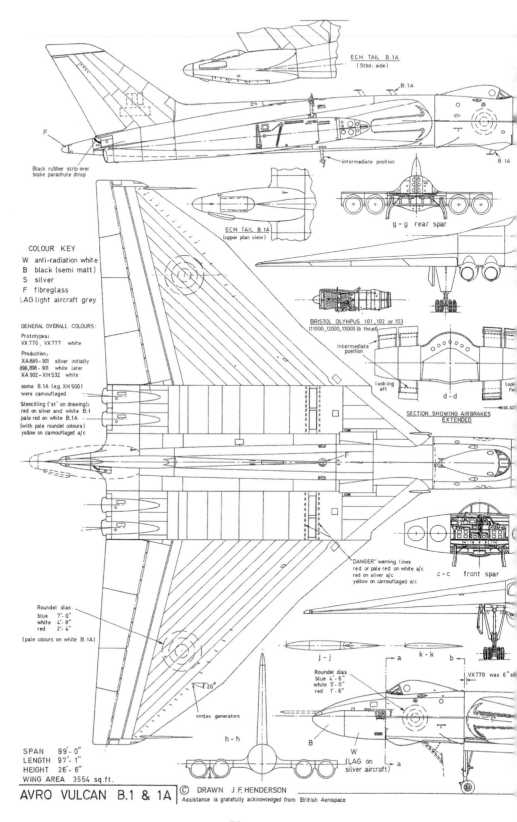

ECM TAIL B.1A
(Stbd. side)

B.1A

F

Black rubber strip over
brake parachute strop

intermediate position

B.1A

ECM TAIL B.1A
(upper plan view)

g – g rear spar

COLOUR KEY

W anti-radiation white
B black (semi matt)
S silver
F fibreglass
LAG light aircraft grey

GENERAL OVERALL COLOURS:

Prototypes:
VX 770, VX 777   white

Production:
XA889–901   silver initially
896,898–901   white later
XA 902–XH 532   white

some B.1A (e.g. XH 500)
were camouflaged

Stencilling ("st" on drawing):
red on silver and white B.1
pale red on white B.1A
(with pale roundel colours)
yellow on camouflaged a/c

BRISTOL OLYMPUS 101, 102 or 103
(11000, 12000, 13000 lb thrust)

intermediate
position

looking
aft

d – d

looking
fwd

SECTION SHOWING AIRBRAKES
EXTENDED

F

"DANGER" warning lines
red or pale red on white a/c
red on silver a/c
yellow on camouflaged a/c

c – c   front spar

Roundel dias.
blue   7'- 0"
white 4'- 8"
red   2'- 4"

(pale colours on white B.1A)

j – j

a   k – k   b

VX770 was 6" s

Roundel dias.
blue   4'- 6"
white 3'- 0"
red   1'- 6"

20°

vortex generators

h – h

B

W

(LAG on
silver aircraft)

SPAN   99'- 0"
LENGTH   97'- 1"
HEIGHT   26'- 6"
WING AREA 3554 sq.ft.

AVRO VULCAN B.1 & 1A

© DRAWN J.F. HENDERSON
Assistance is gratefully acknowledged from British Aerospace

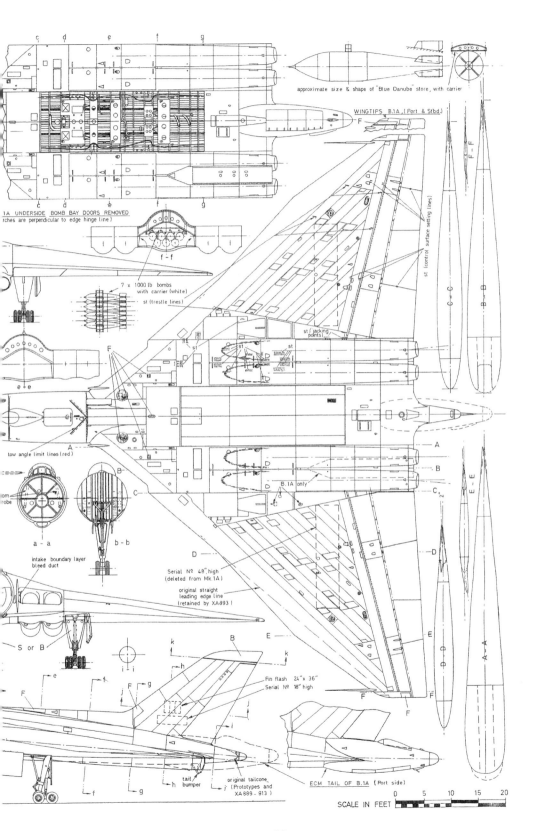

approximate size & shape of "Blue Danube" store, with carrier

WINGTIPS B.1A (Port & Stbd.)

F - F

1A UNDERSIDE BOMB BAY DOORS REMOVED
rches are perpendicular to edge hinge line)

f - f

C - C

B - B

7 x 1000 lb bombs
with carrier (white)

st (trestle lines)

st (jacking
points)

st (control) surface setting lines)

e - e

F

A

A

tow angle limit lines (red)

B

B

C

B.1A only

C

E - E

om
robe

D

D

a - a   b - b

Serial № 48" high
(deleted from Mk.1A)

intake boundary layer
bleed duct

original straight
leading edge line
(retained by XA893)

E

E

S or B

i - i

k

B

E

k

A - A

h

e

f

F   g

F

j

Fin flash 24" x 36"
Serial № 18" high

F

F

f

j

i

tail
bumper

original tailcone
(Prototypes and
XA 889 - 913)

ECM TAIL OF B.1A (Port side)

SCALE IN FEET   0   5   10   15   20

1960

Vulcan B.Mk1A

After delivery back to Woodford on 5 March 1958, XA895 was used as a trials aircraft for the new ECM TI equipment. This led to the Vulcan being redesignated B.Mk1A. It first flew in this configuration on 5 January 1960.

All B.Mk1A conversions were carried out at the Armstrong Siddeley Bitteswell site at Lutterworth, Leicestershire. The first aircraft delivered for conversion were XH500 and XH505, both aircraft being delivered to Bitteswell on 13 July 1959. The B.Mk.1A conversions were completed between 1959 and 1962, with the last deliveries in 1963.

The most visible changes to the B.Mk1A were a flat plate antenna which was fitted underneath between the starboard engine jet pipes, a large refuelling probe to enable in-flight refuelling, and a rear fuselage which accommodated the new radar and electronic countermeasures (ECM) equipment.

Other improvements included the higher-powered Olympus 104 Series engine. The main elements of the electronic suite were the Green Palm voice communications jammer, Blue Diver metric frequency jammer, Red Shrimp centimetric jammer, Blue Saga radar warning receiver and Red Steer rear-facing radar. Decoy chaff dispensers were also fitted. These developments were used for both the B.Mk1A and B.Mk2 aircraft, with variations on those aircraft equipped to launch Blue Steel.

The first two B.Mk1A aircraft delivered to the RAF at Scampton were XH500 and XH505 in September 1960. The last B.Mk1A was delivered to RAF Waddington on 6 March 1963.

XH505 was one of the first B.Mk1 aircraft to be converted to B.Mk1A at Bitteswell. Note the addition of a refuelling probe and enlarged rear fuselage, which housed the ECM equipment.

Vulcan XH503's first flight was on 30 September 1958 and it was delivered to No 44 Squadron on 31 December 1958. It was the last B.Mk1 to be converted to B.Mk1A standard at Bitteswell and was delivered to Waddington on 6 March 1963.

Aircraft Converted to B.Mk1A Standard

XH505 XH500 XH506 XH904 XA912 XH481 XH477 XH483 XH501 XA913 XH504
XH478 XH479 XA907 XH476 XH497 XA909 XA910 XA906 XH482 XH475 XH499
XH532 XH480 XA911 XH502 XH503

B.Mk1A Location of ECM Equipment

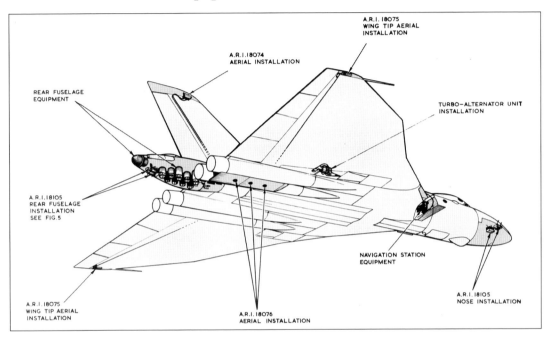

Vulcan B.Mk2 Electronic Countermeasures

It was first proposed in May 1958 to fit a new ECM suite to the Vulcan. This was retrospectively fitted to B.Mk1A aircraft, with the second production aircraft, XH534, being the first B.Mk2 to be fitted with this equipment.

Below left and below right: Pictured on 7 July 1959, XH534 was the first B.Mk2 to be fitted with the new counter-measures suite.

The First and Last XH558

Vulcan XH558 first flew on 25 May 1960 and was the first B.Mk2 delivered to the Royal Air Force on 1 July 1960, to 230 OCU at Waddington.

After XH558 retired from display flying for the RAF Vulcan Display Flight in 1992, it was purchased by C Walton Ltd at Bruntingthorpe.

Due to public demand for XH558 to fly again, the 'Vulcan to the Sky Trust' was formed; this led to XH558 flying again on 18 October 2007. It was finally retired for the last time in October 2015 and is now on static display at Doncaster Sheffield Airport, South Yorkshire. The airport was formally RAF Finningley, where XH558 was based during the 1960s.

XH588 is seen pictured in its early anti-flash colour scheme. Below the fuselage, the Ram Air Turbine (RAT), which was used to provide emergency electrical power in the event of engine failure, can be seen. It is seen here on a systems check. It was also used for ECM trials, and was later converted to the Maritime Radar and Reconnaissance (MRR) and Tanker role.

During the Falklands conflict, XH558 was converted to the tanker role and delivered to 50 Squadron. This was XH558's last role before going to the RAF Vulcan Display Flight in May 1985. It is here seen at Woodford in 1982.

B.Mk1 Vulcan Scramble at RAF Scampton

Vulcan B.Mk1s two-minute scramble at RAF Scampton in 1960. At the time, RAF Scampton was home to 617 Squadron, who made the famous low-level Avro Lancaster dam busting raid in World War Two. The first Vulcan B.Mk1, XH482, was delivered by the Station Commander, Air Commodore J N H Whitford on 6 May 1958.

Below: Vulcan B.Mk1 XH474 crew.

Blue Steel Stand-Off Missile Development

As far back as 1954, the Ministry of Supply (MoS) was aware that Guided Weapons (GW) defence would pose a threat to 'V' bombers flying over, or within, 50 miles of the target by 1960. A note from the MoS stated it would require a flying bomb which would have its maximum use between 1960 and 1965. It was recognised, due to the speed range of Mach 2+, that the production of many vehicles would be required for firing trials and that this would lengthen the development time.

In 1954, Avro employed R H 'Hugh' Francis, who came from the RAE Armament Development Division at Farnborough. Mr Francis, along with his colleagues from the RAE, had worked on various flying bomb and missile designs and was a leading authority in this area. This led to the establishment of a Weapons Research Division at Woodford in 1954 and to a development contract being awarded to Avro in March 1956 for a stand-off missile to meet OR 1132 missile requirement for the 'V' bomber force. The warhead finally chosen was the nuclear fission device known as 'Red Snow'.

Early 19/15 model test missile in Valiant bomb bay.

Scale models were used in the development of Blue Steel with Vickers Valiant aircraft. These models were carried in the Valiant's bomb bay. Further tests completed on B.Mk1 series were powered by the de Havilland Double Spectre rocket engine. The Double Spectre ran on high-test peroxide and kerosene and had two superimposed chambers. The final production Type 100 Series was powered by the Armstrong Siddeley, later Bristol Siddeley, Stentor. It was a two-chamber rocket engine. One chamber was used for initial boost and then a smaller cruise chamber was used for most of the flight.

The Aviation Division of Elliott Brothers (London) Ltd formed in 1953. Based at Borehamwood, they designed the guidance system which was the most advanced type at that time and one of the world's first inertial navigation systems. It was a mixed inertial and Doppler system that gradually corrected the gyro drifts as it approached the launch point. The flight rules computer and autopilot were both developed by Avro. Blue Steel had to fly up to Mach 2+, so the airframe was to be of stainless steel rather than aluminium; this gave Avro new challenges in the production of the missile.

Chadderton and Woodford were involved in the production of Blue Steel. Pictured here is the Blue Steel assembly line at Woodford.

Vulcan B.Mk1 XA903 Blue Steel Development Aircraft

Above: Blue Steel missile pictured at Woodford on 11 November 1960.

In 1960, No 4 Joint Services Trials Unit (No 4 JSTU), was formed at Woodford and arrived in Australia to start testing full scale versions of Blue Steel missile using Valiants, Vulcans and Victors as test vehicles. Round 001 was launched un-motorised on 1 November 1960. Between 1960 and October 1964, over 50 launches were completed, which included high- and low-level trajectory. The main element of the trials unit returned to the UK in November 1964.

Further tests were conducted in the UK by No 18 JSTU, based at Scampton, using Blue Steel aircraft allotted to No 617 Squadron, the first service unit to operate the missile.

Blue Steel test missile at Woodford.

Vulcan XA903 was the only B.Mk1 to carry the Blue Steel missile.

More than 50 operational Blue Steel W105 missiles were delivered to the Royal Air Force, along with W103 training rounds. Sixteen W100A launch capable pre-production rounds were also made available as part of the trials programme, along with eight B.Mk2 aircraft under the control of HQ Bomber Command.

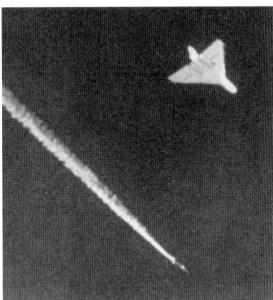

Above left: W100 missile at Boscombe Down on 25 October 1960. Missile engine test firings were completed at Boscombe Down.

Above right: Vulcan XA903 missile test launch.

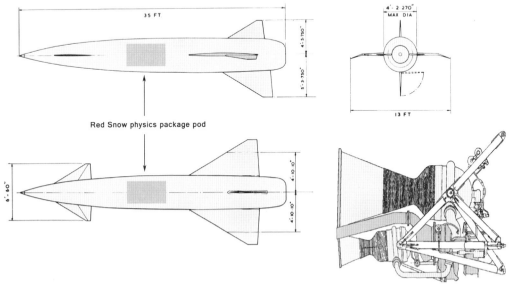

AVRO BLUE STEEL   AIR-TO-GROUND GUIDED MISSILE

OVERALL DIMENSIONS

Dual Chamber Armstrong Siddeley Rocket motor. One chamber was used for initial boost, then the smaller cruise chamber was used for most of the flight. It was fuelled by hydrogen peroxide and kerosene propellant.

Blue Steel Cockpit (Final Conference)

This drawing from the prototype notes for VX770 shows the cockpit in a more conventional configuration to that on the original prototype and later aircraft. The use of an unconventional fighter style single stick control column offered the advantage of saving space within the confines of the cockpit. The Vulcan normally carried a crew of five. First and second pilot, air and electronics officer (AEO), navigator, and nav radar operator. The two pilots had ejection seats and the three rear crew had to rely on their parachutes in an emergency situation. It was also confirmed at the Blue Steel Final Conference on 19–21 December 1960 that the full pressure suit was not being introduced for the B.Mk2 aircraft.

VULCAN (FIRST PROTOTYPE)

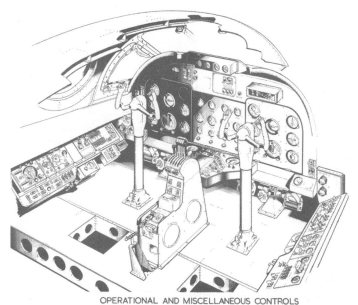

A.L.33

OPERATIONAL AND MISCELLANEOUS CONTROLS

Left: Note the twin pilot's control columns of the original cockpit design. A full size mock-up was also manufactured using this layout.

Below: Pilot's front panels. Note the unconventional fighter style, single stick control columns. Also unique to the Vulcan was the control surface indicator shown in the rectangular case above. It was an added safety feature and represented the tail view of the aircraft. The pilots were positioned above the rear crew, accessed by ladder.

Set operator and Navigator's plotters position. At the time, the Vulcan used the GEE navigation system, which synchronized pulses transmitted from the UK that enabled the navigator to calculate the aircraft's position from the time delay between pulses. It was later replaced in the mid-1960s by the military Tactical Air Navigation system (TACAN) and the American Long Range Navigator (LORAN) system, both of which relied on ground antenna transmitter stations.

Also shown is the CRT screen; above the screen is a camera used for recording the mission and ballistic computing. A joystick was used to move the picture around, it was also connected to the autopilot so that the nav radar operator could steer the aircraft. The Blue Steel inertial guidance system was integrated with the navigation equipment and the nav radar operator would periodically feed in H2S fixes to the missile. Astro navigation was also available by a sextant on either side of the crew's compartment.

Air electronics officer's (AEO) position. The AEO was in charge of all electrical systems and countermeasures equipment. By the time Blue Steel aircraft had entered service, a comprehensive countermeasures suite was fitted.

1961

The above picture shows XH675 Victor Mk2 with a Blue Steel missile taken on 24 August 1961. The Victor XL161 was used as the test aircraft for Blue Steel. It went from Woodford to Australia and was based at Edinburgh airfield.

Missile testing at Woomera, Australia.

Skybolt Ballistic Missile

In May 1960, the British Government agreed to purchase 144 Skybolt missiles from the US. By agreement, British funding for research and development was limited to that required to modify the aircraft to take the missile, with Avro being selected as the UK's main contractor. The first three B.Mk2 Vulcans allocated to be fitted out to carry the Skybolt missile were XH537, XH538 and XL391.

In January 1961, a No 83 Squadron Vulcan went to the Douglas plant at Santa Monica, California, for electrical compatibility tests. The following year, the RAF sent 200 personnel to Elgin Air Force Base in Florida to act as the British Joint Trials Force for advanced testing of Skybolt with a Vulcan B.Mk2.

Close-up of Skybolt missile, 29 September 1961.

Aerodynamic trials were carried out by XH537, seen here with an early version of the Skybolt ballistic missile. On 9 December 1961, XH538 began dummy drop tests over the West Freugh range in Scotland.

High above the Mojave Desert, near California, Avro Vulcan XH535 flies in formation with an American B-52 bomber. Piloted by Tony Blackman and 'Ossie' Hawkins, the Vulcan was in America to take part in tests for Skybolt installation. Like the Avro Vulcan, the B-52 would also carry the Skybolt air-to-surface ballistic missile.

Vulcan B.Mk2 Line-Up Celebrating a Decade of Service

Vulcan B.Mk2 line-up of nine 83 Squadron aircraft at RAF Scampton taken on 11 May 1961. Notice the low visibility markings.

Blue Steel Enters Service

The first B.Mk2 to be delivered to Scampton with a Blue Steel capable missile was XL317 in June 1962. It was given emergency operational capability in August 1962, two months before the Cuban missile crisis in October 1962. It was not until February 1963 that the missile was fully released for service.

Twenty-three production B.Mk2 aircraft were modified to carry Blue Steel, along with three trials aircraft: B.Mk1 XA903, B.Mk2 XH538 and XH539. The production aircraft were fitted with Olympus 201 series engines of 17,000lb thrust and completed between June 1961 and November 1962. These aircraft were XL317, XL318, XL319, XL320, XL321, XL359, Xl360, XL361, XL384, XL385, XL386, XL387, XL388, XL389, XL390, XL392, XL425, XL426, XL427, XL443, XL444, XL445 and XL446.

Alterations included a crank to the front bomb-bay spar, a cut out at the rear spar and new bomb-bay fairings. Modification kits were produced for fitment at RAF bases so that the aircraft could be converted to either a conventional bombing or Blue Steel role.

Operational Blue Steel Vulcan XL320 first flew on 9 November 1961 and was delivered to No 617 Squadron on 4 December 1961. On 30 September 1965, it became part of the Scampton Wing and later went to No 230 OCU on 29 March 1972. It was sold for scrap on 31 August 1981.

In-Flight Refuelling

Another significant development of the B.Mk1A and B.Mk2 was the incorporation of a flight refuelling system. Although proposals for flight refuelling date back to early studies for the Type 698, it was not until 1959 that this facility was tried. Vulcan XH478 was used for testing this system, along with Valiant B1 tanker WZ376 during June 1959 and April 1961. Clearance trials for the B.Mk2 Vulcan were later completed on XH538 during the first three months of 1961.

Flight refuelling significantly increased the range of the Vulcan, as witnessed during the Falkland Islands conflict with Argentina, when XM607 flew from Ascension Island and dropped a full load of bombs on Port Stanley airfield, flying more than 6,600nm in 16 hours. It must not be forgotten that the Vulcan was originally designed as a medium-range bomber without flight refuelling capability.

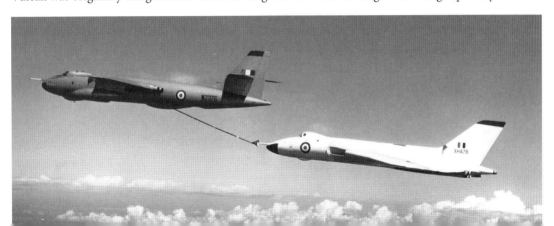

1962

In November 1962, the Americans announced they were cancelling the Skybolt programme. A new replacement plan was hammered out between the two governments, which led to the Nassau Agreement in December 1962, and to the United Kingdom purchasing the Polaris submarine launched ballistic missile system, equipped with British warheads.

The UK would thus retain its independent deterrent force, although its control passed from the RAF largely to the Royal Navy. The RAF kept its tactical nuclear capability.

Avro received notice of the cancellation for 40 Vulcan Mk2 Skybolt aircraft, along with Research and Development work in early January 1963.

Skybolt aerodynamic trial being carried out by XH537. It is seen here on 10 October 1962, with a later version of the redesigned nose re-entry vehicle on the right wing.

Blue Steel Development Aircraft

Vulcans, Victors and Valiants were used in the development of Blue Steel at Woodford on 12 May 1962.

Quick Reaction Alert (QRA)

One of the augments of reverting the nuclear deterrent to the Navy was the vulnerability of the 'V' force to a first strike attack. Along with the adoption of Quick Reaction Alert (QRA), the Vulcan would fly to dispersal bases around the United Kingdom to avoid being destroyed at their main bases but were still vulnerable to a first strike attack.

Quick Reaction Alert was inaugurated in February 1962, with Blue Steel squadrons forming the spearhead of Bomber Command's QRA force and was to do so for over five years. The original procedure was to keep one aircraft from each squadron maintained in an armed condition. Staging points were constructed at the end of the runways, with aircraft parked on short strips to aid rapid take-off.

Vulcan B.Mk2 XL321 of No 617 Squadron with Blue Steel missile pictured on 18 July 1962.

Olympus Development Aircraft

Avro Vulcan B.Mk1 XA894 was allocated to Bristol Siddeley Engines Ltd at Filton for development of the Olympus B.01 22R, which was to be used for the BAC TSR-2 low-level, supersonic reconnaissance and tactical strike aircraft. After arrival at Filton on 18 July 1960, it was converted to carry the 22R engine in a bifurcated pod under the fuselage, and it made its first flight with this engine on 23 February 1962.

Unfortunately, XA894 was destroyed by fire on 3 December 1962, when the under-slung engine shed a low-pressure turbine disc which entered the bomb bay fuel tanks; it had nearly completed eight hours flying time with the Olympus 22R by the time of the accident.

Low-level pass at the Farnborough Air Show by XA894, with the Olympus B.01 22R in a bifurcated pod underneath the fuselage.

Production Orders

An order was placed for 37 B.Mk1 aircraft in September 1954. There were two amendments to this order: amendment one, in April 1956, was for 30 B.Mk1s and seven B.Mk2s; amendment two, in June 1957, was for 20 B.Mk1s and 17 B.Mk2s. A contract for eight B.Mk1 aircraft, placed on 31 March 1955, was amended to eight B.Mk2 aircraft on 1 June 1956, and a contract for 24 B.Mk1s placed on 26 February 1956 was amended on 1 June to B.Mk2s. A final contract was issued for 40 B.Mk2s placed on 22 January 1958. The total number built, including prototypes, was 136.

Development Programme 1957–62

	FLIGHT DEVELOPMENT PROGRAMME				
VULCAN MK.I XA 893	A.C. ELECTRICAL SYSTEM			AERIALS	AWAITING DISPOSAL INSTRUCTIONS
VULCAN MK.I XA 899	MK. IOA AUTO PILOT & MILITARY FLIGHT SYSTEM	AUTOMATIC LANDING TRIALS			
VULCAN MK.I XA 891	B.OL.6 ENGINE DEVELOPMENT				
Ist. PROTO MK. 2 VX 777	HANDLING & DEVELOPMENT		GROUND RIG AT FARNBOROUGH		
VULCAN MK.I XA 895	E.C.M. DEVELOPMENT			DELIVERED TO SERVICE	
Ist. PROD. MK. 2 XH 533	HANDLING & PERFORMANCE				AUTO LANDING
2ND. PROD. MK. 2 XH 534	A&A.E.E. RELEASE TRIALS	MK.IOA AUTO-PILOT		BLUE STEEL	LONG RANGE TANKS
3RD. PROD. MK. 2 XH 535	FINAL CONFERENCE	E.C.M.	SKYBOLT	RADIO TRIALS E.C.M. (WINDOW)	
4TH. PROD. MK. 2 XH 536	RADIO & RADAR		HEADING REFERENCE SYSTEM		
IITH. PROD. MK. 2 XH 557	ENLARGED INTAKES & B.O.L. 301 ENGINES				
12TH. PROD. MK.2 XH 558	E.C.M. (SERVICE TRIALS)	DELIVERED TO SERVICE			
5TH. PROD. MK.2 XH 537	ARMAMENT TRIALS & BOMB BAY FUEL TANKS	SKYBOLT			
7TH. PROD. MK.2 XH 539	BLUE STEEL				
6TH. PROD. MK.2 XH 538	FLIGHT REFUELLING	PREPARATION FOR SKYBOLT			
22ND. PROD. MK.2 XJ 784	B.O.L. 301 ENGINES	MK.2 RAPID T/O SYSTEMS			
4Ist. PROD. MK.2 XL 391	PREPN. FOR SKYBOLT				
	1957	1958	1959	1960	1961	1962

1963

Low-Level Role

When Francis 'Gary' Powers, flying a Lockheed U2 as a covert surveillance aircraft, was brought down near Degtyarsk, Ural Region, of the Soviet Union, by SA-2 Guideline (S-75 Dvina) missiles on 1 May 1960, it became apparent that any high-flying aircraft would be vulnerable to any surface-to-air missile defences. Intelligence reports indicated that this would extend to the 'V' force and a requirement was issued to revert to the less vulnerable low-level role which would delay detection by radar.

Vulcan B.Mk2 XM596 was taken off the production line in 1963 for structural testing, when it was recognised that the resulting fatigue life would be effected by the low-level role. This led to strengthening modifications to enable the Vulcan to have a longer fatigue life of 12,000 hours. These structural modifications were completed at Bitteswell under a future remediable programme.

With the Valiant being phased out in 1964 due to metal fatigue, and the Victor not being suitable for the low-level role, it was left to the Vulcan to fulfil this requirement with its inherent stronger structure, capable of withstanding the buffeting experienced at low level.

New Camouflage Scheme for the Low-Level Role

The first B.Mk2 Vulcan to have the new low-level camouflage scheme was XM645; it was to have a dark green and medium sea grey upper surface and white anti-flash underside. The aircraft were usually given a glossy Polyurethane finish. Particular attention was paid to giving the white underside a smooth finish and all rivets were made flush and any gaps were filled in. In the early 1970s, some aircraft were given a light grey lower surface, and the black radome began to disappear, as part of a general toning down.

When the Vulcan was manoeuvring at low-level, it was found that the white anti-flash underside was clearly visible, so the Vulcan adopted an overall matt 'satin' camouflage scheme to make it less visible at low-level. In 1977, two aircraft were a given a disruptive desert camouflage of sand and stone on the under surface for the 'Red Flag' exercise in the United States.

Blue Steel was converted so it could be launched at low-level; this significantly affected the range of the Blue Steel missile. Pictured is XL320, taken on 16 December 1966, seen in its low-level camouflage scheme.

1964

Production of the Vulcan finished in 1964, with 17 being delivered that year. The final production Vulcans were transferred to the newly formed Cottesmore Wing, which was formed by relocating No 9, 12 and 35 Squadrons in November 1964. All Cottesmore Wing squadrons operated the Yellow Sun Mk2 free fall nuclear bomb at that time.

Avro Vulcan XL446 in low-level camouflage scheme. The aircraft was first flown on 16 November 1962 and went to No 27 Squadron at Scampton on 31 November. Note the two flat plate antennas between the engine nacelles, which were fitted to most Blue Steel aircraft. It is seen here on 17 September 1964.

With the cancellation of Skybolt, and the United Kingdom's nuclear deterrent reverting to the Royal Navy in 1962, the Vulcan continued with Blue Steel until the end of 1969. The Vulcan continued in the more conventional role, but still kept its nuclear capability. Shown below is XM649 at low-level on 16 June 1966.

The Vulcan Years, 1952–64

Build list and first flights of the Avro Vulcan

In summary, the last production Vulcan was built in 1964. Shown below are the first flight dates of every Vulcan built.

Aircraft	First Flight
1952	
VX770 1st Prototype	30 August
1953	
VX777 2nd Prototype	3 September
1954	
1955	
XA889 B.Mk1	4 February
XA890 B.Mk1	24 August
XA891 B.Mk1	22 September
XA892 B.Mk1	23 November
1956	
XA893 B.Mk1	16 January
XA895 B.Mk1	12 August
XA897 B.Mk1	10 July
XA898 B.Mk1	26 November
1957	
XA894 B.Mk1	9 January
XA896 B.Mk1	30 January
XA899 B.Mk1	16 February
XA900 B.Mk1	7 March
XA901 B.Mk1	19 March
XA902 B.Mk1	13 April
XA903 B.Mk1	10 May
XA904 B.Mk1/A	31 May
XA905 B.Mk1	26 June
XA906 B.Mk1/A	19 July
XA907 B.Mk1/A	21 August
XA908 B.Mk1	28 August
XA909 B.Mk1/A	20 September
XA910 B.Mk1/A	22 October
XA911 B.Mk1/A	31 October
XA912 B.Mk1/A	13 November
XA913 B.Mk1/A	26 November
XH475 B.Mk1/A	19 December

1958		
XH476 B.Mk1/A		8 January
XH477 B.Mk1/A		29 January
XH478 B.Mk1/A		14 July
XH479 B.Mk1/A		1 March
XH480 B.Mk1/A		21 March
XH481 B.Mk1/A		8 April
XH482 B.Mk1/A		16 April
XH483 B.Mk1/A		1 May
XH497 B.Mk1/A		15 May
XH498 B.Mk1		6 June
XH499 B.Mk1/A		23 June
XH500 B.Mk1/A		12 July
XH533 B.Mk2**		30 August
XH501 B.Mk1/A		21 August
XH502 B.Mk1/A		4 October
XH503 B.Mk1/A		31 October
XH504 B.Mk1/A		30 November
XH505 B.Mk1/A		8 December
	1959	
XH506 B.Mk1/A		20 January
XH532 B.Mk1/A		25 March
XH536 B.Mk2**		3 May
XH534 B.Mk2**		18 June
	1960	
XH557 B.Mk2**		2 April
XH535 B.Mk2**		7 May
XH558 B.Mk2**		25 May
XH559 B.Mk2**		29 June
XH537 B.Mk2**		4 August
XH560 B.Mk2**		30 August
XH561 B.Mk2**		17 September
XH562 B.Mk2**		21 October
XH563 B.Mk2**		1 November
XJ780 B.Mk2**		28 November
	1961	
XH538 B.Mk2**		4 January
XJ781 B.Mk2**		10 January

XJ782 B.Mk2**	16 January	XM599 B.Mk2*	30 August
XJ783 B.Mk2**	3 February	XM600 B.Mk2*	6 September
XH554 B.Mk2**	18 February	XM601 B.Mk2*	21 October
XJ784 B.Mk2*	9 March	XM602 B.Mk2*	28 October
XJ823 B.Mk2**	30 March	XM603 B.Mk2*	15 November
XJ824 B.Mk2**	24 April	XM604 B.Mk2*	15 November
XH539 B.Mk2**	10 May	XM605 B.Mk2*	22 November
XH555 B.Mk2**	9 June	XM606 B.Mk2*	28 November
XL317 B.Mk2**	24 June	XM607 B.Mk2*	29 November
XJ825 B.Mk2**	7 July	XM608 B.Mk2*	24 December
XL318 B.Mk2**	11 August		
XH556 B.Mk2**	31 August	**1964**	
XL319 B.Mk2*	1 October	XM609 B.Mk2*	2 January
XL320 B.Mk2**	9 November	XM610 B.Mk2*	22 January
XL321 B.Mk2**	6 December	XM611 B.Mk2*	23 January
		XM612 B.Mk2*	13 February
1962		XM645 B.Mk2*	25 February
XL359 B.Mk2**	10 January	XM646 B.Mk2*	16 March
XL360 B.Mk2**	31 January	XM647 B.Mk2*	2 April
XL361 B.Mk2**	21 February	XM648 B.Mk2*	17 April
XL384 B.Mk2*	16 March	XM649 B.Mk2*	28 April
XL385 B.Mk2*	30 March	XM650 B.Mk2*	12 May
XL386 B.Mk2*	2 May	XM651 B.Mk2*	1 June
XJ387 B.Mk2*	16 May	XM652 B.Mk2*	16 July
XL388 B.Mk2*	25 May	XM653 B.Mk2*	14 August
XL389 B.Mk2*	13 June	XM654 B.Mk2*	2 October
XL390 B.Mk2*	3 July	XM655 B.Mk2*	2 November
XL392 B.Mk2**	19 July	XM656 B.Mk2*	25 November
XL425 B.Mk2**	6 August	XM657 B.Mk2*	21 December
XL426 B.Mk2**	13 August		
XL427 B.Mk2**	14 September		
XL443 B.Mk2**	18 September		
XL444 B.Mk2**	12 October		
XL445 B.Mk2**	30 October		
XL446 B.Mk2**	16 November		
XM569 B.Mk2*	11 December		
1963			
XM570 B.Mk2**	31 January		
XM571 B.Mk2**	31 January		
XM572 B.Mk2**	9 February		
XM573 B.Mk2**	27 February		
XM574 B.Mk2*	28 March		
XM575 B.Mk2*	19 April		
XL391 B.Mk2*	14 May		
XM576 B.Mk2*	16 May		
XM594 B.Mk2*	4 June		
XM595 B.Mk2*	4 July		
XM596 B.Mk2	**Fatigue testing**		
XM597 B.Mk2*	12 July		
XM598 B.Mk2*	15 August		

** Olympus 201 series * Olympus 301 series

XM607, XM612, XM597 and XM598 were the Black Buck aircraft used in the Falklands conflict in 1982, these aircraft used the Olympus 301 series engines.

VX770 taken on 1 July 1953.

Early Development Flights

Following its first public demonstration flights in September 1952 at Farnborough, VX770 carried out its initial programme of test flying. Shown below are the flights made by the first and second prototype Vulcans during the early development programme between 1952 and 1953.

1952

Date	Description	Flight
29/8/1952	First taxi test. Evening taxi too late for flight	–
30/9/1952	First Flight – Saturday	1
01/9/1952	To Boscombe Down	2
01/9/1952	Undercarriage retraction	3
02/9/1952	Undercarriage functioning	4
02/9/1952	SBAC Air Show aircraft based at Boscombe Down	5
04/9/1952	SBAC Air Show aircraft based at Boscombe Down	6
05/9/1952	SBAC Air Show aircraft based at Boscombe Down	7
06/9/1952	SBAC Air Show aircraft based at Boscombe Down	8
07/9/1952	SBAC Air Show aircraft based at Boscombe Down	9
08/9/1952	SBAC Air Show aircraft based at Boscombe Down	10
09/9/1952	SBAC Air Show aircraft based at Boscombe Down	11
3/11/1952	Ground undercarriage functioning	–
12/11/1952	Ground undercarriage functioning	–
24/11/1952	Undercarriage functioning flight. Trim curves	12
10/12/1952	Undercarriage functioning flight	13
10/12/1952	Landing. Take-offs & undercarriage functions	14
11/12/1952	Simulated power control failures	15
12/12/1952	Take-offs and landings etc	16
18/12/1952	CG limits etc	17
21/12/1952	Trailing static PEs (Pressure Error Tests). Stalls etc	18
24/12/1952	PEs	19
29/12/1952	PEs runs	20
30/12/1952	Accelerated & decelerated no specific tests	21
31/12/1952	Familiarisation Boscombe Down pilots	22
31/12/1952	Familiarisation Boscombe Down pilots	23

1953

1953 saw the first flight of the second prototype Vulcan VX777 and carried on the further development of the Vulcan.

Date	Description	Flight
18/02/1953	Familiarisation Boscombe Down pilots	24
19/02/1953	High Speeds	25
20/02/1953	Demonstration	26
24/02/1953	High Mach numbers trace recordings	27
24/02/1953	High Mach numbers trace recordings	28
25/02/1953	High Mach numbers oscillations trace recorder	29
26/02/1953	High altitude PEs	30
26/02/1953	High altitude PEs	31
26/02/1953	Meteor A/O Vinten K and handheld A4 camera	32

Date	Description	No.
28/02/1953	High altitude PEs. Airbrake failure	33
27/06/1953	General handling. Sapphire engine	34
27/06/1953	General handling	35
30/06/1953	General handling	36
01/07/1953	General handling	37
09/07/1953	General handling	38
09/07/1953	General handling & Demonstration Flypast	39
09/07/1953	Demonstration Flypast	40
10/07/1953	Demonstration Flypast	41
10/07/1953	Tank bay pressures	42
13/07/1953		43
14/07/1953	Take-offs and Landings	44
14/07/1953	Familiarisation – Avro Test Pilot Jack Wales	45
15/07/1953	Queens review Royal Air Force	46
23/07/1953	Engine bay pressures	47
23/07/1953	Level speeds	48
25/07/1953	Stretton Naval Air Show	49
03/08/1953		50
06/08/1953	Demonstration with CAA & ARB	51
12/08/1953	Aneroid PEs at Boscombe Down	52
12/08/1953	Aneroid PEs at Boscombe Down	53
12/08/1953	Aneroid PEs at Boscombe Down	54
12/08/1953	Aneroid PEs at Boscombe Down	55
18/08/1953	Parachute stream	56
19/08/1953	Demonstration	57
19/08/1953	Demonstration	58
19/08/1953	Demonstration	59
19/08/1953	Demonstration	60
20/08/1953	Strain gauges wing spars & taxi tests	61
01/09/1953	Zone 2 engine bay tests	62
03/09/1953	**First flight second prototype (VX777)**	**1**
03/09/1953	Demo, Air Marshal Sir John Baker	63
03/09/1953	Stick Force through trim range	64
04/09/1953	General handling (VX777)	2
04/09/1953	General handling (VX777)	3
05/09/1953	SBAC rehearsal	65
05/09/1953	SBAC rehearsal	66
07/09/1953	General handling (VX777)	4
08/09/1953	SBAC Air Show (VX777)	5
09/09/1953	SBAC Air Show (VX777)	6
09/09/1953	SBAC Air Show (VX777)	7
10/09/1953	SBAC Air Show (VX777)	8
11/09/1953	SBAC Air Show (VX777)	9
12/09/1953	SBAC Air Show (VX777)	10
13/09/1953	SBAC Air Show (VX777)	11
13/09/1953	SBAC Air Show (VX777)	12
13/09/1953	SBAC Air Show (VX777)	13
14/09/1953	SBAC Air Show (VX777)	14
06/09/1953	SBAC Air Show	67
07/09/1953	SBAC Air Show	68
08/09/1953	SBAC Air Show	69
09/09/1953	SBAC Air Show	70
11/09/1953	SBAC Air Show	71

12/09/1953	SBAC Air Show	72
13/09/1953	SBAC Air Show	73
14/09/1953	SBAC Air Show	74
14/09/1953	SBAC Air Show	75
16/09/1953	SBAC Air Show demonstration (VX777)	15
16/09/1953	SBAC Air Show demonstration	76
17/08/1953	Transit to Boscombe Down (VX777)	16
17/08/1953	Familiarisation Boscombe Down pilots (VX777)	17
17/08/1953	Familiarisation Boscombe Down pilots (VX777)	18
17/09/1952	Engine failure at start of take-off (VX777)	19
22/09/1953	Airbrake positions & strain gauges	77
22/09/1953	Drag measurements	78
22/09/1953	Drag measurements	79
22/09/1953	Drag measurements	80
22/09/1953	Drag measurements	81
28/09/1953	Transit from Boscombe Down (VX777)	20
29/09/1953	Demonstration (VX777)	21
01/10/1953	Calibration (VX777)	22
02/10/1953	Strain gauges, airbrakes etc	82
07/10/1953	Strain gauges	83
07/10/1953	Strain gauges	84
07/10/1953	Strain gauges	85
08/10/1953	Strain gauges	86
14/10/1953	Pull outs	87
15/10/1953	Airbrakes vibration vibrographs	88
16/10/1953	Engine runs	
19/10/1953	Airbrakes vibration vibrographs	89
22/10/1953	Trailing static tests	90
03/12/1953	Calibrations	
06/12/1953	Calibrations	
17/12/1953	Ground run	
19/12/1953	Calibration trimmers	
20/12/1953	Elevator artificial feel calibration	
21/12/1953	Airbrakes	91
23/12/1953	Change of trim with airbrakes	92

Second prototype Vulcan VX777 with VX770 in the background at Woodford flight sheds in September 1953.

Olympus Engine Development

The design of the Olympus series of engines can be traced back to a Bristol Aircraft Division requirement in 1946 for a high thrust engine of 9,000lb thrust. The design was for a long-range, high-flying bomber, designated Type 172. Engine specification T.E.1/46 was issued by the Bristol Engine Division to meet this requirement. The first engine ran on 6 May 1950, designated the B.01.1; it weighed 3,600lb and gave a thrust of 9,140lb. By November 1950, B.01 1/2 was running on a test bed producing a thrust of 9,500lb.

The second prototype Vulcan, VX777, made its first flight on 3 September 1953 with four Olympus series 100 engines, which had been re-engineered from the derated Olympus 99 that had powered the high-altitude, record-breaking English Electric Canberra. Engine trials with the Olympus series 100 had begun in the summer of 1952, with flight clearance being given in January 1953 at a lowly rating of 9,250lb thrust.

The first production Olympus for the Vulcan was the Mk101, which produced 11,000lb thrust at an overall ratio of 10.2.1; it received its type test certificate in December 1952. The 101 was up-rated to 12,000lb thrust and re-designated the 102. By raising the turbine entry temperature, it was found that a gain of 1,000lb thrust could be achieved, and a conversion was made to all existing 102 engines, which were up-rated to 104 standard.

The 104 was initially rated at 13,000lb thrust, type tested at that rating in December 1956 and flew for the first time in XA889. The aircraft had been delivered to Filton for development work on the 104 in July 1957. When the 104 entered service in the Vulcan B.Mk1, it had a rating of 13,500lb.

A further development for the Vulcan was the Olympus 200 series, which was designed in parallel with the first production examples; the first of these engines, the B.01 6, developed 16,000lb of thrust.

The Olympus 200 started life under the designation B.01 6. It first ran at Bristol Siddeley Engines Patchway factory in September 1954; later, a developed version the B.01 7 produced 17,000lb of thrust. These new engines were fitted to XA891 at Filton in spring 1958, but development with this aircraft stopped when, on a test flight from Woodford, it crashed because of total electrical failure in 1959.

The first Olympus 200 engine flew in the first production Vulcan B.Mk2 XH533 on 19 August 1958. The final engines used on the Vulcan were the Olympus 201 and 301 versions. With the requirement for more thrust, the Olympus 201 (B.01.21), was developed with a thrust rating of 17,000lb, which first ran at the Patchway factory in January 1959. The second B.Mk2 (XH534) was equipped with Olympus 201 engines of 17,000lb thrust in 1959 and used for A&AAE trials.

By this time, in 1959, Bristol Aero-Engines Ltd had merged with Armstrong Siddeley Motors Ltd and became known as Bristol Siddeley Engines Limited (BSEL). In 1966, Bristol Siddeley was purchased by Rolls-Royce.

A new Olympus Type 301 (B.01.21A) was designed to give an increase in thrust of 20,000lb. With the increase in thrust, Avro designed intakes to accept the larger capacity of the new engine. Vulcan XH557 had been allotted to BSEL for the new engine installation. So that the larger B.01.21A could replace the 201 Olympus engines on XH557, structural alterations had to be made to the airframe, and XH557 flew for the first time with the new engine on 19 May 1961; it was then delivered to Woodford for handling assessment trials.

Avro also converted XJ784 to accept four Olympus 301 engines and the aircraft went to the A&AAE in April 1962 for initial CA release trials. Following a limited clearance, the 301 finally entered service with the RAF in June 1963.

When the Series 201 entered service, it was to encounter problems of engine surging mainly with the inboard engine at medium to high altitude and this led to attempts by Avro to improve the airflow at the intake. The aircraft used for these trials was XH560. The surge problem was finally solved by a cut back of the LP turbine stators by 2 per cent and that, combined with a revised fuel system schedule, resulted in surge free handling. A notable difference between the 201 and 301 was the wider and shorter tail cone of the Olympus 301. The Olympus 301 finally entered RAF service in June 1963 with a limited clearance of 18,000lb. It was restored to the original rating for Operation *Black Buck*.

Olympus Development Timescale

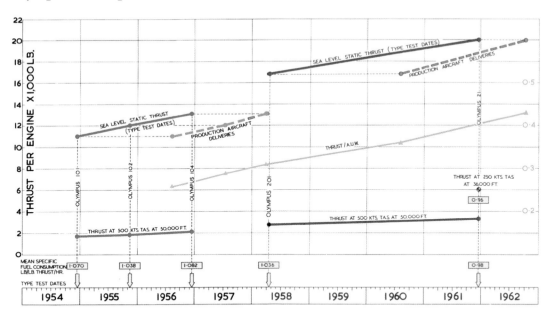

Olympus 101 Turbojet – Starboard View

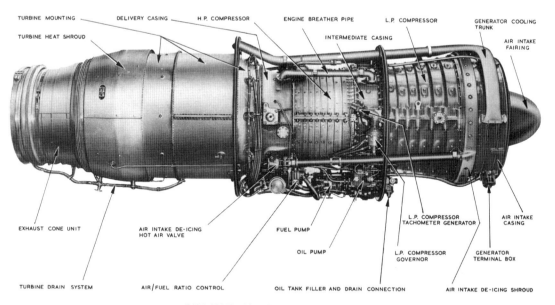

OLYMPUS 101 TURBOJET — STARBOARD VIEW

The Bristol Olympus jet engine was continuously developed for the Vulcan. The first production engine, the Olympus 101, produced 11,000lb thrust, and, by 1962, the 201 Series Olympus was giving 17,000lb of thrust and the Olympus 301 was producing 20,000lb of thrust.

Vulcan General Data

Vulcan B.Mk1 (Straight Wing) July 1954 Brochure

B.Mk1
General Dimensions

Length overall	97ft 1in
Span overall	99ft
Height (dimension approximate due to tyre and oleo deflection)	26ft 6in
Wheel base	29ft 2in

B.Mk1A
General Dimensions

Length overall (from nose) 99ft 11in (from refuelling probe)	105ft 6in
Span overall	99ft 5in
Height (dimension approximate due to tyre and oleo deflection)	26ft 6in
Wheel base	29ft 2in

Wing

Aspect ratio	2.76
Gross wing area	3,554sq ft

Vulcan B.Mk2 – March 1968 Brochure

Normal gross weight	190,000lb
Normal cruising speed	500kts
Cruising altitude	45,000–65,000ft
Bomb capacity: normal	10,000–30,000lb
Range (10,000lb bomb or 13,000lb special store)	5,000–5,500nm
Range (photo-reconnaissance)	5,850–6,110nm

General Dimension

Length overall (from nose) 99ft 11in (from refuelling probe)	105ft 6in
Span overall	111ft
Height (dimension approximate due to tyre and oleo deflection)	27ft 1in

Wing

Aerofoil section	RAE.104, 5 per cent modified
Chord (mean)	35.712ft
Chord (root)	63.4ft

Power Units x 4	Olympus 201, 202 or 301

Weights

Prior to production set 41 maximum permissible all up weight (AUW)	180,000lb
Maximum permissible AUW with plus Mod No 1302, 1309, 1321 and 1334	190,000lb
Maximum permissible AUW with plus Mod No 1456, 1587, and 1627	195,000lb
Maximum permissible AUW (overload case)	210,000lb
Maximum permissible Landing Weight (overload case)	210,000lb
Maximum Normal Landing Weight	195,000lb

Three View General Arrangements

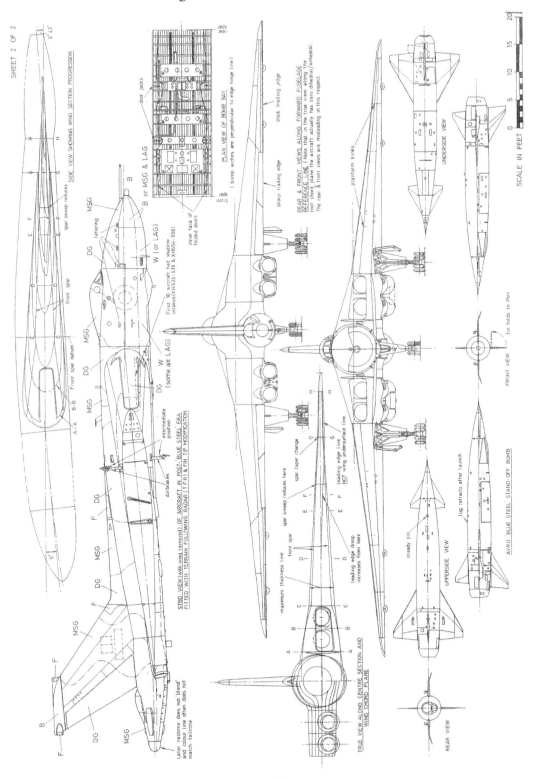

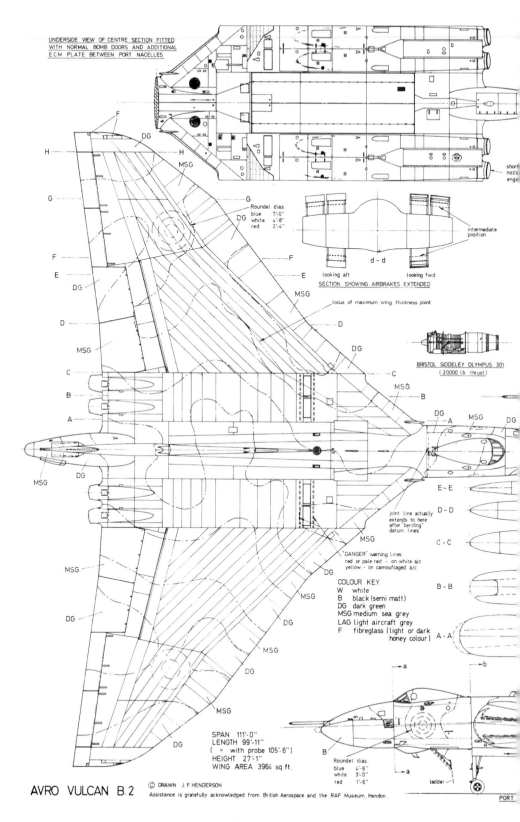

UNDERSIDE VIEW OF CENTRE SECTION FITTED WITH NORMAL BOMB DOORS AND ADDITIONAL ECM PLATE BETWEEN PORT NACELLES

Roundel dias.
blue 7'-0"
white 4'-8"
red 2'-4"

looking aft   looking fwd
SECTION SHOWING AIRBRAKES EXTENDED

intermediate position

d – d

locus of maximum wing thickness point

BRISTOL SIDDELEY OLYMPUS 301
(20000 lb. thrust)

joint line actually extends to here after 'bending' datum lines

"DANGER" warning lines
red or pale red – on white a/c
yellow – on camouflaged a/c

COLOUR KEY
W   white
B   black (semi matt)
DG dark green
MSG medium sea grey
LAG light aircraft grey
F   fibreglass (light or dark honey colour)

SPAN   111'-0"
LENGTH 99'-11"
(" with probe 105'-6")
HEIGHT 27'-1"
WING AREA 3964 sq.ft.

Roundel dias.
blue 4'-6"
white 3'-0"
red 1'-6"

ladder

PORT

AVRO VULCAN B.2

© DRAWN J.F HENDERSON
Assistance is gratefully acknowledged from British Aerospace and the RAF Museum, Hendon.

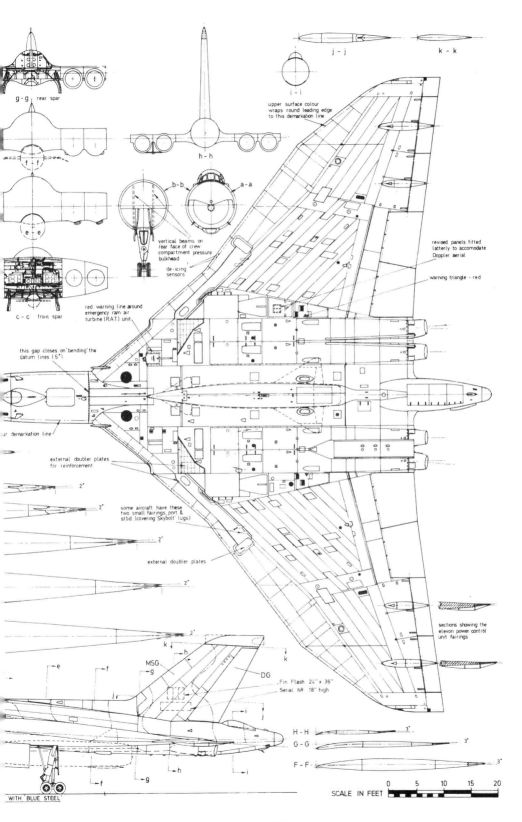

g - g   rear spar

f - f

e - e

C - C   front spar

h - h

b - b   a - a

vertical beams on
rear face of crew
compartment pressure
bulkhead

de-icing
sensors

j - j

k - k

i - i

upper surface colour
wraps round leading edge
to this demarkation line

revised panels fitted
latterly to accomodate
Doppler aerial

warning triangle - red

red warning line around
emergency ram air
turbine (R.A.T.) unit

this gap closes on 'bending' the
datum lines (5°)

demarkation line

external doubler plates
for reinforcement

some aircraft have these
two small fairings, port &
stbd. (covering 'Skybolt' lugs)

external doubler plates

sections showing the
elevon power control
unit fairings

k

h

MSG
g

k

DG

e   f

Fin Flash 24" x 36"
Serial Nº 18" high

j

j

H - H

G - G

F - F

e   f

g   h   i

f   g   h

WITH 'BLUE STEEL'

2°

2°

2°

2°

2°

3°

3°

3°

SCALE IN FEET   0   5   10   15   20

89

End of an Era

By 1982, there were only three Vulcan squadrons remaining, Nos 44, 50 and 101, all based at RAF Waddington. The last operational Vulcan squadron was 50 Squadron, which was disbanded for the last time in March 1984, 20 years after the last Vulcan B.Mk2 made its first flight.

Black Buck Raids

During the Falklands War in 1982, the Vulcan completed five missions of the seven planned. Victor K2 tanker aircraft were used for the air-to-air refuelling of the Vulcan and were, along with the Vulcan, based on Ascension Island in the South Atlantic.

The first raid (Black Buck 1) was on 30 April–1 May 1982, when a 44 Squadron Vulcan, XM607, piloted by Flight Lieutenant Martin Withers and his crew, successfully dropped 21 1,000lb bombs on Port Stanley Airport. The last mission (Black Buck 7) was also performed by Martin Withers and his crew on 12 June using XM607, and two days later the Argentinian ground forces surrendered. Black Buck missions 2, 5 and 6 were completed by XM598.

These raids were the longest bombing missions made by the RAF at that time and a triumph of logistics and planning. It was the first and last time the Vulcan was used in anger.

Pictured is XM575 of No 44 Squadron (Rhodesia) over its base at RAF Waddington on 10 August 1982, just two months after the Falklands conflict had ended on 14 June 1982. Note the shorter and wider tail cone used for the Olympus 301 engine.

To Sum Up

It is interesting to note the comparison with the original OR229 and OR230 for a long-range bomber. It is also often overlooked that the Air Staff originally specified a requirement to fly at low-level. This was deleted from the original OR requirement because it would have eliminated any high aspect wing.

Operating Requirement OR230

In 1947, Avro found that the B35/46 Delta wing design could achieve the range called for in OR230; although at a lower altitude over the target, but at the speed of 500kts, it appeared of interest to know what size Delta wing aircraft would be required to meet this requirement in full — that is to say, to raise the operating altitude from 46,500ft to 50,000ft at the target and to have full load factors.

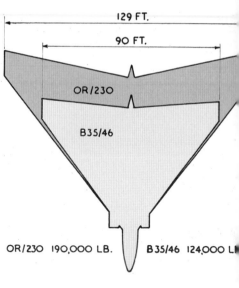

The answer was somewhat startling, as it brought the gross weight up to 190,000lb. This appeared to be a heavy price to pay for an increase in altitude of 3,500ft at the target. The 230 Operating Requirement would require four jet engines of 15,000lb static thrust each, compared with the B35/46 (OR229) requirement for four 9,410lb static thrust engines.

The final version of the Vulcan had a wingspan of 111ft 0in, had more powerful Rolls-Royce Olympus 301 engines that could develop 20,000lb static thrust and had a maximum take-off weight of 204,000lb.

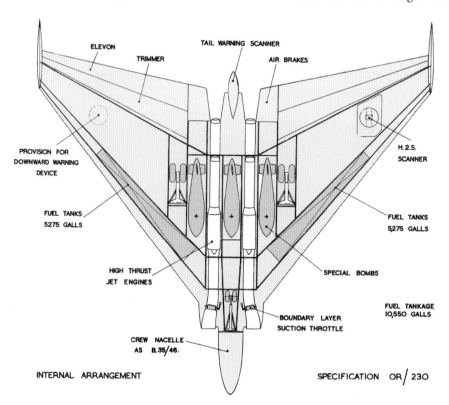

The mammoth task of getting the first Vulcan squadron into service with the RAF required a total of 39,500 drawings, from the start of the Type 707 series to completion of the basic Vulcan, and 1,467,000 drawing office man-hours. Other statistics included the following: a total of 50,000 special tools and 167,063 separate parts (excluding engines, nuts, bolts, rivets, etc)

Each Vulcan contained 410,300 nuts, bolts, washers, etc; metal sheet sufficient to cover 1.5 football pitches; 9,362ft of tubing; 14 miles of electric cable and 2.5 miles of rolled sections. In addition to the Avro production line, 17 sub-contractors built airframe parts. A total of 39,000 bought-out items were involved, from more than 400 suppliers.

For two years, teams of Avro specialists ranging from test pilots and engineers to teachers, artists, and writers were engaged on the job of getting the Vulcan into RAF service. The company's technical publications department had written and produced three volumes of lecture notes, a 1,200-sheet spares schedule, two volumes (1,000 pages) of descriptive and maintenance notes, teaching aids and pilot's notes.

A special instructional school at Woodford trained RAF instructors, technicians, engineers and pilots on airframe instrument maintenance and electrical systems.

Above right: On 25 July 1981, the RAF celebrated 25 years of the Vulcan in service at RAF Scampton. The flying display included a four-aircraft scramble. A year later, the Falkland Islands conflict started on 2 April 1982.

Vulcan Squadrons and Bases

No 9 Squadron	Conningsby 1962–64; Cottesmore 1964–69; Akrotiri 1969–75; Waddington 1975–82
No 12 Squadron	Conningsby 1962–64; Cottesmore 1964–67
No 27 Squadron	Scampton 1961–72; 1973–82
No 35 Squadron	Cottesmore 1964–69; Akrotiri 1969–75; Scampton 1975–82
No 44 Squadron	Waddington 1960–82
No 50 Squadron	Waddington 1961–84
No 83 Squadron	Waddington 1957–60; Scampton 1960–69
No 101 Squadron	Finningley 1957–61; Waddington 1961–82
No 617 Squadron	Scampton 1958–81
No 230 OCU	Waddington 1956–61; Finningley July 1961–69; Scampton 1969–81

Station units adopted an aircraft pooling policy in 1964. Waddington had already used aircraft pooling pre-B.Mk2. Individual markings resumed in 1972, with a few exceptions.

Vulcan Survivors

Pictured on its last flight, Avro Vulcan XM603 flew from Waddington to Woodford on 12 March 1982. The aircraft first flew on 19 November 1963 and was delivered to No 9 Squadron at RAF Conningsby on 3 December 1963. It served with Nos 9, 27 and 50 Squadrons before ending its career with 44 (Rhodesia) Squadron at Waddington. The last operational flight was on 28 February 1982, and, at that time, it had flown more than 5,732 hours. It can now be seen at the Avro Heritage Museum in an all-white, anti-flash colour scheme used in the high-level role.

VULCAN XM603

Note the thimble under the refuelling probe used for the terrain following radar. Also on top of the fin is the ARI 18228/1 Radar Warning Receiver.

Above left and above right: XM603 when supported by the XM603 club members. Pictured above, right, is XM603 at the Avro Heritage Museum at Woodford, still in its all white anti-flash colour scheme, but with low visibility markings and black radome.

XH558	Robin Hood Airport, Doncaster. Taxiable
XJ823	Solway Aviation Museum, Cumbria
XJ824	Imperial War Museum, Duxford
XL318	Royal Air Force Museum, London
XL319	North East Aircraft Museum, Sunderland
XL361	Goose Bay, Canada
XL426	London Southend Airport. Taxiable
XM573	Strategic Air and Space Museum, US
XM575	East Midland Aeropark, Castle Doninington, Leicestershire
XM594	Newark Air Museum
XM603	Avro Heritage Museum, Woodford
XM605	Castle Air Museum, US
XM607	RAF Waddington, Lincoln, Lincolnshire
XM612	City of Norwich Aviation Museum
XM655	Wellesborne, Warwickshire Mountford Airfield. Taxiable

Above left: As mentioned earlier, XH558 was the first B.Mk2 to enter RAF service and, due to public demand, returned to the air show circuit performing for the public for seven years before being retired in 2015. It is seen here, flying over Woodford for the last time on 27 June 2015, 55 years after its first flight. It last flew in October 2015. It can now be seen at Robin Hood Airport, Doncaster.

Above right: XM575 seen flying over Lincoln Cathedral flown by Flt Lt Martin Withers of Falkland War fame on 19 August 1982. It can be seen at the East Midland Aeropark, Castle Donington, Leicestershire.